FRENCH BLOOMS

FRENCH BLOOMS

floral arrangements inspired by paris and beyond

SANDRA SIGMAN
founder of
Les Fleurs
Floral, Home, Garden

———

written with Victoria A. Riccardi

Foreword by Sharon Santoni

Principal photography by Kindra Clineff
with additional photography
by Anne Soulier and Abigail Matses

RIZZOLI
NEW YORK

New York · Paris · London · Milan

This book is dedicated to my dear friend Kindra, for always chasing the light with her camera, and to my mom, for inspiring me to believe that my dreams were achievable.

—*Merci de tout mon cœur*
(Thank you with all my heart)

CONTENTS

FOREWORD

Sandra and I first met at an antiques fair outside of Paris. We were obviously shopping for the same kinds of items, and from this simple first encounter a friendship was born. It did not take long to understand that we shared a passion for gardens and flowers, and although our growing seasons may differ slightly—I live in Normandy and she lives in New England—we are able to grow the same plants on opposite sides of the ocean.

Sandra understands the power of flowers, and—having lived in France—she wanted to share the magical French way of designing blooms back home in the United States. In French cities, windows and balconies are often colored with flowers, or even decorated with elegant topiary. In the country, the humblest of gardens can offer lilacs in the spring, and roses in the summer. In household potagers, you often see flowers growing between the rows of cabbages or tucked in beside tomatoes. The potager becomes a cutting garden, as well as a source of food for the home.

In France, the options for buying flowers are multiple. Even the smallest village or town will boast at least one florist. Buckets of flowers are displayed outside shopfronts, encouraging potential buyers to choose their own blooms before venturing inside to discover what other wonders may be available.

At farmer's markets, vendors bring bunches of seasonal varieties from their own gardens: lilacs in the spring, zinnias and sweet peas in the summer, and dahlias in the fall. They place their bunches in jugs and pitchers of water, and a customer who comes to buy carrots, eggs, and other foodstuffs can simply add a touch of color to their purchases.

Flower displays do not have to be intricate or huge. A large bouquet makes a fantastic statement piece, but stem vases containing single blooms dotted around a dining table can be every bit as eloquent.

The joy that it gives Sandra to work with flowers and to create stunning displays for her clients is wonderful to see. And maybe even greater is the pleasure that she finds in teaching floral art. Giving tips and guidance, sharing her own wealth of experience, and helping others to find their own styles are things she and I share during the workshops we host in Normandy and Provence.

Ultimately, flowers—be they growing in a garden or displayed in a vase—are made for sharing. Sandra has devoted her professional life to sharing her own passion for flowers and is known for her signature color palette and elegant, French-inspired style. During the pandemic, when flower producers were struggling and Sandra could not allow her employees to come into work, she continued to share her flowers. She committed to supporting her suppliers and showing love to her community. She made bouquets, alone in her store, and drove them to care homes and other places where people were in need of comfort and left the bouquets in front of their doors.

Those who know Sandra can bear witness to how generously she shares her love of flowers in her everyday life. This beautiful book will broaden that circle and allow her to share with a wider audience of true flower lovers . . . be they in Paris or elsewhere.

—*Sharon Santoni*

INTRODUCTION

I fell in love with flowers thanks to my mom, who began her own floral business in my childhood home in New England. Although I never saw myself as creative, I regularly offered to help my mom out, especially when she had a lot of orders, such as during the holidays. I secretly hoped that she would consider the flowers I created worthy, and over time I knew she did, as I perfected my techniques under her guidance.

My casual interest in helping my mom arrange flowers blossomed into a full-blown obsession when I moved to France in my early twenties. Growing up, I had trained as a figure skater and had the opportunity to ice skate professionally with *Holiday on Ice* in Paris. There, I saw flower shops unlike any I'd ever seen. These *fleuristes* (florists) overflowed with lush blooms—in pots and urns by the entrance and by the armful in vases inside the store. In one particular shop called Les Fleurs, I befriended the staff and began learning the secrets of French floral design. Little did I know this experience would pave the way to what I do now.

After a year and a half of living in Paris, I was ready to go home. My mother's breast cancer had returned, and I wanted to be with her. I thought if we could open a flower shop together, like Les Fleurs in Paris, she would have a reason to keep living. We plotted and planned for months and in January 1989 opened our little French flower shop together. As fate would have it, my mom passed away a month later. Although I was a frightened twenty-three-year-old girl with no business experience, I knew I had to move forward. So, mustering the same grit and determination I used during my skating career, I decided my *fleuriste* would be my mom's legacy.

Thirty years later, Les Fleurs is still thriving in a much larger space, where my design team and I create French-inspired flower arrangements and sell new and vintage French home and garden goods. Flooded with sunlight, the shop brims with treasures I bring back from annual buying trips to France. We also have a flower bar, displaying all our fragrant blooms in tall containers, just like the shops in Paris. My workroom lies in the back, where my staff and I design arrangements for life's big and small moments, even wearing the same long black aprons those young women wore at Les Fleurs in Paris. I also hold floral workshops in the studio, as well as in Provence and Normandy, every spring and fall. During these moments, I share with each attendee the skills they need to create French-inspired florals at home. Now, I share those same skills with you.

I have organized this book to be both inspirational and practical. The first part opens with gorgeous vistas of Paris—the charming flower shops, the Paris wholesale flower market, and blooming gardens—all of which planted the first seeds for my opening of Les Fleurs.

Next, I share my approach to arranging flowers with a French accent, following the time-honored design principles I learned in that French flower shop. From there, I discuss how to choose the right size, color, and container style for your blooms because in France and at Les Fleurs, not just any vase will do. After that, I cover things you'll need to know and have on hand for arranging your flowers, such as tools and how to plant a French cutting garden in your own style.

Next, I explain how to create over twenty seasonal arrangements with a French twist via easy-to-follow instructions and photos. For example, I explain how to make floral arrangements for your dining room table, kitchen counter, and mantelpiece. As you'll see, these arrangements aren't fussy or overdone, and each one can be scaled back or elevated to fit your needs.

I hope this book inspires you to bring a little bit of France into your home, the same way those French flower shops inspired me to open Les Fleurs and eventually to write this book. *Bon chance.*

PARIS

where it all began

I came to Paris to figure skate professionally and left with a dream—to open a Parisian-style
flower shop with my mom. I never will forget that
first visit, when the city captured my heart from the
moment I arrived. I remember calling home and telling
my mom how the bridges were sheathed in gold
and topped with sculptures. The architecture was
the most beautiful I'd ever seen—Gothic churches,
Baroque-style residences, and massive tree-lined
boulevards crisscrossing the Seine. The cafes
brimmed with people relaxing outside sipping coffee
from china, not paper cups to go. Small side streets
led to secluded courtyards, cobbled squares, and
hidden gardens. This city had intrigue, beauty, and
style unlike anything I'd ever encountered before.

Since my skating performances were at night,
I spent my days exploring the city. At first, I visited museums, cafes, and neighborhood bistros.
Eventually, I began ducking into flower shops, which
were so different from the ones in America. Instead of
bare, commercial-looking entrances, these *fleuristes*
had shiny painted exteriors with plants and flowers
spilling onto the sidewalks. The interiors abounded
with masses of flowers arranged by color. Think
bundles of fuchsia sweet peas, nestled between pink,
long-stemmed roses and blush-colored flowering
quince. These elegant blooms were out in the open
for everyone to see them and smell their fragrance,
unlike the flowers back home, which sat in buckets in
back refrigerators.

My favorite florist sat at the bottom of my street,
Rue Saint-Lazare, near the Opéra. It was called
Les Fleurs and became my second home. The
staff—mainly young women—were so friendly and
welcoming that I began hanging out with them. I
didn't speak much French, but I knew the language
of flowers, and soon I was helping around the shop,

wearing the same long black apron as the designers. I swept the floor, cleaned and prepped the blooms, and helped in whatever way I could, not for pay, but for the sheer joy of being around flowers and people who loved them.

Over time, I began absorbing these women's unique approach to arranging flowers. I saw blooms I'd never encountered before, even though I often accompanied my mom to our massive floral whole-saler in Boston. Rushed for time, my mom had a more grab-and-go mentality. If the flowers seemed fresh and the right color, we were done. I never saw her take additional time to look for perfect bunches or venture off to find something new. We were there to get what was needed and race back home to design as quickly as possible. (Although I now chuckle at our approach, these were some of the fondest moments I shared with my mom and the memories I treasure most.)

I learned about Rungis, the wholesale flower market on the outskirts of Paris, where most florists buy their flowers and foliage. The young women I had befriended didn't use common fillers in their bouquets. They tucked in exotic greenery, like wands of rosemary. I discovered how to choose the best container for each kind of arrangement and make a hand-tied bouquet. Another surprise—whenever a client entered Les Fleurs, a designer would work with them. What sort of colors do you like? What type of occasion are you planning? It was the first time I realized how a client and floral designer should work together to create an arrangement. The more time I spent helping out at Les Fleurs, the clearer it became that this was the kind of flower shop my mom and I would open together.

When I wasn't at Les Fleurs, I strolled around gardens, like the Jardin des Tuileries, the Jardin du Luxembourg, and lesser-known spots, like Parc de Bagatelle, known for its roses. I noticed what color combinations the French used for their plantings, the types of greenery that set off their bulbs, and the seasonal varieties of annuals they planted. Eventually, all this would inform my own French-style cutting garden.

ABOVE LEFT: *The Medici Fountain in the Jardin du Luxembourg.* ABOVE RIGHT AND OPPOSITE: *Spring roses flourish in the Parc de Bagatelle, in the heart of the Bois de Boulogne, filled with statues and arched floral walkways.*

Sadly, Les Fleurs in Paris no longer exists. But on my annual buying trips to France, I visit other favorite florists. Take Flamant, for example, tucked away in the sixth arrondissement. This charming shop with a black awning feels like an enchanted garden with florals beckoning you in from the sidewalk and crowding the aisles. Flamant sells an abundance of beautiful, beribboned, hand-tied bouquets, like the ones I teach you to craft in this book. Then, there is Stéphane Chapelle, where the namesake owner creates displays for fashion brands, such as Chanel and Louis Vuitton. Nestled behind the Palais Royal, his hunter-green shop has a dramatic, museum-like interior showcasing masses of seasonal blooms and small tablescapes, similar to the ones I tell you how to make for your home. I also love Clarisse Béraud of Maison Vertumne near Tuileries, who carefully selects the color and type of bloom to tell her client's "story."

All these designers take a bespoke approach to floral design and value quality florals over quantity, a way of working with flowers that has deeply informed what I do at Les Fleurs.

On these trips back to France, I also visit *brocantes* (flea markets and vintage and antiques shops) where I buy containers for my floral arrangements and goodies for the store. For example, at different vintage markets, like the Marché aux Puces at Porte de Vanves on the outskirts of Paris, I spend several days dipping in and out of stalls hunting for treasures. I search for woven French baskets in which to cradle florals in a vase. I look for the pedestal vases that inform so many of my floral designs. I hunt for French white ironstone jugs, pitchers, and teapots, along with French transferware pieces, including soup tureens. All these antique pieces look stunning filled with flowers. I also seek old copper and zinc watering cans, vintage

champagne buckets, and green blown-glass demi-johns to repurpose as vases.

Then, of course, I stop by Rungis. Aside from seeing its massive selection of blooms, I visit the area selling garden antiques. I search for cast-iron planters, along with ceramic urns and old French crocks, to hold arrangements. After two weeks of treasure hunting, newly inspired by all I have seen, I ship everything home via container to my little French flower shop.

Ever since I began my floral business, I've noticed that the French aesthetic touches people's hearts in the same way it touched mine many years ago. I hear that all the time from my floral clients and workshop participants, including those who attend my workshops in Normandy and Provence. What resonates with them all is the chic yet nonchalant style of French floral design that evokes a romantic, enticing way of life. And now, it's a life I get to experience more deeply. Not long ago, my husband and I decided to look for an apartment in Paris. On a Friday we saw six listings, none of which spoke to us. Then, my husband went online and found a sunny abode in the sixth arrondissement.

We convinced the agent to show us the apartment, despite it being a Saturday, when brokers usually don't work. Exhausted from jet lag, I didn't check the address but simply put myself in my husband's hands. As we neared the listing, I began to get butterflies. We were in my favorite neighborhood. Then, suddenly, the taxi turned down my favorite street and stopped. I couldn't believe it. The apartment was spacious, sunny, and even more exquisite than I could have imagined. We made an offer on the spot, and it's now ours. We can visit Paris often and I plan to teach floral workshops and give tours with trips to flea markets. I am probably getting ahead of myself, as all this is for another book. But my life has come full circle. Having fallen in love with Paris as a young woman, my secret hope of one day living there has come true.

SECRET SPACES

some of my favorite gardens

Since Paris is my second home, it's no surprise that I have accumulated a list of favorite places, such as where to buy French-girl cashmere sweaters and enjoy the ultimate steak frites. I also have a list of beloved gardens, flower shops, and antiques markets, which I share throughout this book. Below are the gardens that I love to stroll through, especially when they're filled with blooms.

JARDIN DES PLANTES

5th arrondissement

———

Founded in 1625 as a royal garden of medicinal plants, this sixty-eight-acre oasis also houses Paris's oldest zoo, a school of botany, and a natural history museum. I enjoy strolling the grounds to see the incredible bounty of breathtaking blooms and plants.

JARDIN DES TUILERIES

1st arrondissement

———

These gardens, which separate the Louvre Museum from the Place de la Concorde, take their name from the tile factories formerly located on the site. Queen Catherine de' Medici chose to build the Palais des Tuileries here in 1564. André Le Nôtre, the heralded gardener for King Louis XIV, re-landscaped the gardens in 1664 in today's formal French garden style. I particularly love these gardens in early spring when the pink magnolia trees are in full bloom.

PARC DE BAGATELLE

16th arrondissement—Bois de Boulogne

———

The park and its château were built in sixty-four days in 1775 based on a wager between Queen Marie-Antoinette and her brother-in-law the Count of Artois. It is one of the City of Paris's four botanical gardens and a hidden gem. My favorite part of the park is the stunning rose garden composed of 10,000 rosebushes in more than 1,200 varieties.

GIVERNY GARDENS

Eure, Normandy

———

It takes only one and a half hours by train to travel from Paris to Giverny, where artist Claude Monet lived and created two charming gardens. The Clos Normand garden contains masses of flowers, fruit trees, and climbing roses, while the Japanese-inspired water garden has bridges, weeping willows, and waterlilies. The gardens served as inspiration for many of Monet's paintings.

JARDIN DU LUXEMBOURG

6th arrondissement

———

Queen Marie de' Medici, the widow of King Henry IV, commissioned the construction of this majestic garden in 1612 when she moved her residence from the Louvre to Luxembourg Palace. The garden's design took inspiration from the Boboli Gardens in Florence, where Medici was born. I love seeing all the colorful blooms, shady footpaths, and the central pond circled with those quintessentially Parisian sage-green metal chairs. This garden still takes my breath away every time I visit.

EPHRUSSI DE ROTHSCHILD VILLA AND GARDENS

Saint-Jean-Cap-Ferrat, Provence-Alpes-Côte d'Azur

———

Nine glorious themed gardens lie nestled around the Ephrussi de Rothschild Villa: French, Spanish, Florentine, Japanese, a lapidary garden, an exotic garden, a rose garden, and gardens dedicated to Provence and Sèvres.

french floral

DESIGN

principles

When it comes to style, the French seem to have been born with it. Whether we're talking about fashion, home design, or flowers, they exhibit what I can only describe as a sophisticated chicness with a *soupçon* of casualness and understated grace. Whether you're in the heart of Paris or Provence, you see it everywhere, from the whitewashed country kitchens filled with collected cutting boards to the elegant neck scarves that remain perfectly in place. It's a unique and utterly irresistible style and one that defines my way of arranging flowers.

The French buy flowers as if they were selecting cheese for a dinner party. I'm not kidding. Instead of rushing into a florist and grabbing a premade bunch of flowers (which they'd seldom find), they enter knowing what sort of arrangement they want and where it's going in their home. Then, they and the florist choose only the finest-quality specimens that are regionally sourced and at their peak to create an arrangement with the perfect size, shape, and colors—just as I do at Les Fleurs with my clients.

French florists rarely carry anything out of season, in the same way authentic French restaurants only offer, say, asparagus in spring, chestnuts in the fall, and root vegetables in winter. The wholesale flower stalls of Rungis, where most Parisian florists buy their blooms, support this tradition with their supremely seasonal offerings. For example, in early May, they sell multiple varieties of peonies. When peony season in France ends, approximately nine weeks later, that's it. When I went shopping for flowers with my mom, she used to buy whatever was available—in season or not. But when I lived in Paris, I saw the glaring difference between peak-season florals versus out-of-season ones. Take tulips, for example, which are at their peak in spring. They have large petal heads, and you'll find an immense variety. Come summer, the choice of

OPPOSITE: *A bountiful Paris bouquet sits wrapped and ready for purchase, while masses of spring flowers sit on display at the wholesale Rungis floral market.* ABOVE: *In the northwest town of Bellême, France, Gabrielle Feuillard sells chic floral arrangements and accessories.*

varieties and quality of the heads have begun to fade with the heat. The same holds true for dahlias. The ones that bloom in early summer are less hearty and vibrant than those that flourish in the fall.

When it comes to color choice, French florists tend to work in specific color palettes, often all warm- or all cool-colored blooms. If they mix colors, they

tend to choose no more than three; otherwise, the bouquet will look too busy. These similarly hued arrangements, like mine, grace the home with an understated elegance.

Regarding the shapes of their arrangements, French florists rarely follow the traditional floral designs taught at most flower arranging schools,

like pyramids and balls. Instead, working with specific containers and chosen florals and foliage, the French build each bouquet as if it were a bespoke work of art, adding a sprig of this and that to create an organic, three-dimensional whole. Each arrangement is unique and doesn't follow a cookie-cutter design because no two flowers are alike.

French florists rarely use humdrum flowers, like daisies, pungent lilies, gladioli, and baby's breath. Why? These flowers are grown in abundance and would detract from the overall masterpiece. Instead, they look for unusual seasonal varieties and let each flower's intrinsic quirks and qualities add structure, rhythm, and texture to the final display, along with complexity and surprise. The French embrace imperfection because it adds individuality. Think about a bouquet of long-stemmed red roses. You'd rarely see that in France. That's because the commonality of only red roses makes it hard to showcase any design creativity. Instead, the French take a monochromatic approach and combine a few red roses with other similarly hued florals in, say, burgundy, magenta, and dark pink. The result is a more exciting and ultimately stunning bouquet.

The French add texture and contrast to their arrangements by juxtaposing flowers and greenery. For example, they might set off smooth elements, like lush, green hosta leaves, with nubby ones, like hyacinth buds or a branch of unripe blackberries. A round sprig of sweet William might pair with a spray of lisianthus. A spiky mass of sea holly might be softened with cashmere-like lamb's ear.

They inject rhythm into their arrangements by placing flowers and foliage in ways that encourage the eye to move all around the finished piece. This means using round and linear flowers and cutting flowers in different lengths to place them high and low in the arrangement. Like the French, I love to create larger

Adriane M. Fleuriste Paris in the seventh arrondissement is notorious among floral connoisseurs for its gorgeous blooms and bouquets. Fans include the American food maven Ina Garten, who loads up on the shop's flowers when visiting the city.

pedestal arrangements that have movement via their asymmetric shape. I do this by first arranging the foliage so that one side is higher than the other. Then, I insert the flowers along the same upward curve as the foliage, eventually creating a three-dimensional whole. Repeating colors, textures, and shapes also can add movement, along with adding what I call "dancers." These are blooms, like scabiosa, that have a sort of wavy bounce to them. I like to add a few dancers to the arrangement's lowest part, so the flowers almost look like they're falling out of the container.

You also can add liveliness to a bouquet by inserting some curling, reaching, and radiating elements, such as corkscrew hazel, sprigs of pussy willow, or bells of Ireland. One of my favorite ways to create a sense of spriteliness to a tablescape is to march small bud-filled cordial glasses or vases down the center of a dining table interspersed with votives. Alternating the size, form, and color of the plant material in the bud vases further engages the senses in a fun and playful way.

Another element of French floral design is to edit the arrangement when it's nearly complete to give it an airy, romantic looseness. This means pulling out greenery that's blocking certain flowers and removing specific blooms that are crowding the arrangement. You also want to make sure each bloom is facing out. This is particularly important with flowers like dahlias.

The final secret touch is to add a unique visual *bonbon*, which I sometimes refer to as focal or face flowers. I learned this from my French flower shop mentors. For larger designs, it could be a rare or special bloom, like some gorgeous peonies, to elicit an "Oh, look!" sense of delight. Since odd numbers tend to be most pleasing, I usually add three, five, or seven of these *bonbons* to each arrangement, depending upon its size.

ABOVE: *A riot of rosy hydrangea and pink, white, and magenta dianthus entice Parisian passersby.* **OPPOSITE:** *Oz Garden Pour Flamant in the sixth arrondissement looks right out of a fairy tale with its artfully arranged bouquets, blooms, and alluring in-store floral vignettes.*

FRENCH FLORAL DESIGN PRINCIPLES

~1~
Buy the highest-quality, seasonally available flowers and greens, avoiding humdrum varieties, which will detract from the artistry of your bouquet.

~2~
Choose a suitable container for your florals (see Part Three: All About Containers, page 45), based on the number of flowers you're working with, where the arrangement will go in your home, and the current season.

~3~
When selecting flowers for your bouquet, choose either warm- or cool-colored blooms to create an elegant, monochromatic look. If mixing colors, use no more than three.

~4~
Approach each floral composition as if it were a bespoke work of art, adding a sprig of this and that as you go, to create an organic, pleasing whole.

~5~
Add texture and contrast for interest and complexity.

~6~
Embrace imperfection, because no two flowers are the same and, thus, no two arrangements will be the same.

~7~
Inject rhythm for liveliness and movement.

~8~
Tuck in unexpected greenery for surprise appeal.

~9~
Edit your composition, knowing less is more.

~10~
Finish by adding a sweet floral treat.

SECRET SPACES

some of my favorite flower shops

Whenever I am in Paris, I stop by certain flower shops and greet the owner with a kiss on each cheek. These florists have become my friends and I love catching up on their lives and seeing their latest designs. Surrounded by masses of fragrant blooms, posies, ribbons, and seasonal floral displays, these shops not only inspire me, but are where I'll treat myself to a hand-tied bouquet.

ADRIANE M. FLEURISTE PARIS
4 Rue Saint-Dominique, 75007

———

This *fleuriste* is located on the corner of Rue Saint-Dominique and Rue de Bellechasse in the seventh arrondissement. With its expansive floral displays outside, you can't miss it. Peek inside and you'll be delightfully overwhelmed with the masses of flowers and plants.

L'ARROSOIR
80 Rue Oberkampf, 75011

———

This 100-year-old flower shop is now owned by a fellow American, Adrienne Ryser, who fell in love with France, a French man, and flowers. When the shop's previous owners retired, she jumped at the opportunity to acquire it. Every time I visit, the shop bursts with beautiful blooms and intoxicating scents.

MAISON VERTUMNE
12 Rue de la Sourdière, 75001

———

Visit the chartreuse-painted Maison Vertumne in the heart of the first arrondissement of Paris to see why clients have been coming back to Clarisse Béraud and her prestigious shop for over twenty years. Her arrangements are voluptuous and exquisitely made with luxurious, seasonal flowers.

OZ GARDEN POUR FLAMANT
8 Rue de Furstemberg, 75006

———

Located in the Saint-Germain des Prés district near the sweet Musée Delacroix, this gem of a florist is on the other side of the high-end home goods store Flamant. The shop boasts some of the prettiest florals in all of Paris. The last time I was in the square by the shop, I was surrounded by flowers and serenaded by an opera singer.

———

Helpful Hints When Buying a Bouquet *à la Française*

Visit your favorite *fleuriste* on restock day, which is typically Saturday morning, for the freshest flowers.

Invited to a French dinner? Always bring flowers as a form of appreciation.

When buying a bouquet for a gift, mention that it is *pour offrir* (to gift) and the shop will wrap your bouquet with a pretty bow.

Stay away from mostly all-white bouquets, as they are generally for weddings. Instead, create a bouquet with complementary hues that will translate into a clean and elegant design.

———

all about

—

CONTAINERS

I f you're like most people, you think that almost any vase in your cupboard can hold your bouquet. But as I learned from the French, choosing the right container is an art.

First, you want to decide where the arrangement will go, because that will inform your vase's style and size. For example, a spacious front hall table can handle a much larger vase and arrangement than a powder room. And a sleek white living room with modern furniture will call for a different sort of vessel than what you'd put in a Victorian-style salon brimming with antiques.

Next, you want to figure out how big you want your finished arrangement to be. Are you creating a bouquet for your kitchen island? If so, you'll want the arrangement scaled appropriately so that it doesn't overwhelm the space or hit the ceiling lights. It happens. So often, people think they need a towering vase for an island. But tall vessels often have large openings, which require specific-size bouquets. To be aesthetically correct, your floral composition should be almost twice the size of its vase. I am all for tall arrangements in the right setting, but most of the time, a lofty display is just too much for your home and better suited to a hotel lobby.

You also want to think about the vase's color. If you have a bouquet of cool-toned florals, like blues, purples, and lavenders, you will want to choose a cooler-toned vase, such as one in gray or taupe. Flowers in a warm palette, like coral, cream, and raspberry, call for a warmer-toned vase. Choosing a vase in the same color family as the flowers is chic, elegant, and very French.

Topiaries, French pottery, vintage goods, and garden delights all on display inside Les Fleurs in Andover, Massachusetts.

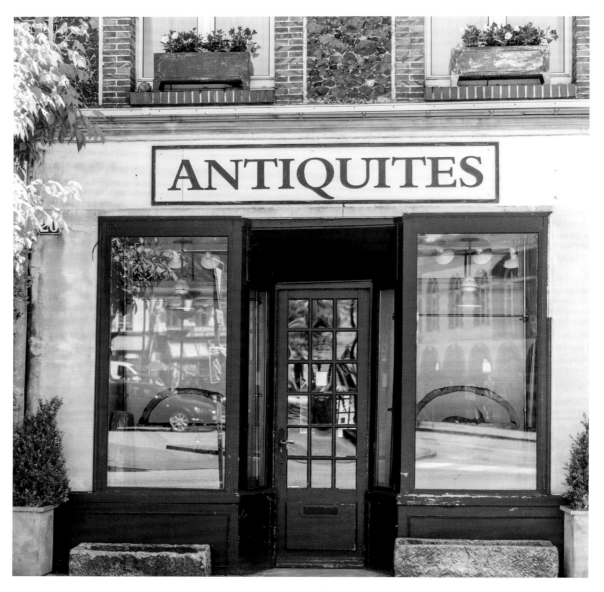

ABOVE AND OPPOSITE: *Antique stores in Normandy, Paris, and Provence offer old-world treasures—from wheelbarrows and watering cans to lion garden statues and cream crockery.*

Seasonality is another element you'll want to consider when choosing your holder. For example, spring's pastel-colored blooms look best in glass and pale-colored holders. But the darker, jewel-toned florals of autumn and winter look best in dark or metallic containers. To see a white vase in the middle of October can be jarring. The French simply wouldn't do that.

Finally, there are times when the vase takes center stage and you want to showcase it. This is often the case with a holder that has an intricate pattern or combination of colors. In that case, the flowers should be very simple, so they don't steal the limelight.

Many of the vessels I use and sell at Les Fleurs come from France, because those are the ones that

best support my floral style. One of my favorites is the pedestal urn, which has an opening wider than the base and allows me to create arrangements that appear to dance and almost float above the container. I also love the French country look of putting bouquets in rustic holders, like French mustard jars and antique stoneware crocks. I encourage you to do that, too. The French respect artisanal items that show the hand of the maker. So don't forget to raid your cupboards for heirlooms and hand-crafted containers. Using your favorite creamer, teapot, or even dessert coupe as a vase gives the arrangement personality. Plus, every time you pull out these containers, you are reminded of when and where you got them.

Ultimately, you're better off having a few treasured holders instead of masses of nondescript vessels, including commercial glass cylinders, cubes, bubble bowls, and pinched-neck vases left over from previous arrangements. Having too many vases can feel overwhelming, and the commercial ones will sap your bouquets of character (so consider giving them away). At the Parisian flower shop where I hung out, several regular clients used to bring their own vases. I noticed over time that these French women had only two or three holders, but each one was absolutely gorgeous (and probably quite expensive). These women would arrive with the one vase they wanted to fill and leave with just the right bouquet. When it comes to vases, less is more.

OPPOSITE AND LEFT: *Baskets, vintage galvanized flower buckets, white pottery vases, and brown-glazed water pitchers are French country brocante finds perfect for holding flowers.*

OBJETS

here are the french-style containers
I use most often for my arrangements

SMALL AND MEDIUM PEDESTAL-STYLE URNS

These vessels are perfect for mantelpiece and coffee table arrangements, since their wide mouths encourage romantic, loose displays that move vertically.

FOOTED CRYSTAL, MARBLE, OR METAL COMPOTES

The shallow, wide-mouth shape of these vessels makes them ideal for lush, elongated arrangements to display on commodes, sideboards, and front hall tables.

IRONSTONE TUREENS & PITCHERS

The heft and casual nature of these creamy white containers make them ideal for holding tall blooms and foliage. They also work well for less formal arrangements set on kitchen counters and entry tables.

SMALL BOTTLES, VASES, GLASSES & JARS

Bud-filled mustard pots, cordial glasses, inkpots, small vases, and creamers all look perfect in small areas of your home, such as a powder room, on a windowsill, or on a bedside table. You can even arrange a collection of these small flower-filled vessels trailing down a dining room table interspersed with votives to give you a big bang for your floral buck.

WHITE CERAMIC FOOTED VASES

With a flared opening, this container style is perfect for frothy arrangements that spill over the sides in a carefree, feminine way and to put on guestroom bureaus, mantels, and side tables.

UNCONVENTIONAL OPTIONS

Have fun and put your blooms in offbeat containers, like a vintage copper watering can or fancy crystal compote. They'll give your arrangement a sense of surprise and whimsy. Plus, it's a good excuse to pull out and enjoy a treasure you normally keep tucked away.

BASKETS

Depending upon its shape, one of these woven containers (with a vase placed inside to hold the water and blooms) looks at home in a vestibule, in a sunroom, or on a kitchen island.

SECRET SPACES

some of my favorite antiques markets

Below are favorite antiques markets that I visit for business and pleasure. Some are open only part of the year, while others are open on weekends. The number of merchants at each market varies and each one tends to draw me for specific items. Regardless, nothing beats the thrill of finding that perfect piece of Paris history in the form of a serving spoon, cordial glass, or pedestal vase that I buy for either myself or my store.

LE MARCHÉ AUX PUCES DE PARIS SAINT-OUEN

110 Rue des Rosiers, 93400
Saint-Ouen
pucesdeparissaintouen.com

———

Founded in 1870, this flea market consists of twelve covered markets and draws the largest concentration of antique and secondhand dealers globally. The markets are open every weekend of the year from Friday through Monday. Insider's info: Arrive early, since it gets more crowded in the afternoon. I always swoon at the stunning chandeliers and mantels.

VIDE-GRENIERS

vide-greniers.org

———

Vide-greniers translates to "attic emptier." Every arrondissement in Paris regularly hosts these flea markets. To find one near you, visit the website. Also, this type of market is often advertised with posters that are tacked up throughout the neighborhood where it is to be held.

LE MARCHÉ AUX PUCES DE LA PORTE DE VANVES

5 Avenue de la Porte de Vanves, 75014
visitparisregion.com/en/portes-
de-vanves-flea-market

———

Nearly 400 merchants sell their wares at this year-round weekend flea market held every Saturday and Sunday from 7 a.m. until 2 p.m. Strolling around the market and digging for treasures makes for a fun morning. You'll find a large variety of well-priced antiques.

LA FOIRE DE CHATOU

On the outskirts of Paris
foiredechatou.com

———

This is the oldest and largest fair in France and occurs twice a year—in March and at the end of September. The fair runs for over a week and attracts vendors from across France and Europe to sell their precious finds. I never leave empty-handed. A tip: Arrive hungry because the fair also has a history of celebrating the eating of *jambon* (ham), which is available from the many pop-up restaurants.

ST. SULPICE FAIRE

Place Saint- Sulpice, 75006 Paris

———

Place Saint-Sulpice turns into a flea market once a year for twelve consecutive days. Discover stunning antiques from collectors and great artisans.

L'ISLE-SUR-LA-SORGUE ANTIQUES MARKET

L'Isle-sur-la-Sorgue,
Provence-Alpes-Côte d'Azur

———

If you're an antiques lover like me and up for a weekend trip to Provence, you must visit L'Isle-sur-la-Sorgue, an idyllic town on the Sorgue River that's second only to Paris when it comes to sourcing antiques. Every Easter and Feast of Assumption (August 15), the town hosts an international antiques fair. And every Sunday (8 a.m. to 6 p.m.), it welcomes over 300 antiques dealers selling everything from birdcages and garden statues to vintage linens and porcelain from Limoges.

flower arranging

—

BASICS

Choosing the flowers and greenery to put in your vase is half the fun of creating an arrangement. Below, I offer sources for both, along with instructions for cleaning and conditioning your plant material to prolong its life. I also provide a list of basic tools and materials you'll find handy when creating my French Floral Recipes, see page 85. Finally, I'll explain how to cultivate your own French-style garden, since it will provide the freshest blooms you can grow, along with unusual varieties not often sold retail.

Good Sources for Your Flowers and Foliage

Several factors can influence where you get your blooms, including the size, color, and style of the arrangement you'd like to make. One of your best floral sources is your own garden, if you have one. You can plant annuals and perennials in all your favorite varieties and colors, adding berries, grasses, and other greenery to lend excitement to your garden and bouquets. At Les Fleurs, much of what I use comes from my French cutting garden. I grow light blue and pink hydrangea, along with an ivory lacecap variety, which starts off a creamy white and then turns pinkish in late summer. I love to add lacecap hydrangea to our wedding florals, since it has such an elegant, feminine look. I also grow different colors of Dutch tulips, all kinds of roses, bluish globe thistles, and clematis, which has beautiful purple blooms and fluttery green leaves. I also cultivate frilly, pale amethyst scabiosa, along with lily of the valley and pieris, a spring shrub with frothy flowers, in my case, white. Of course, French lavender is a must in my garden, along with patches and pots of herbs, including mint, rosemary, and purple sage.

For foliage, I have lots of different varieties of hosta, along with rhododendron, which has long-lasting, shiny oval leaves that I just love to use in arrangements. I also have smoke bush, which creates these frothy, feathery flowers in autumn. I grow a variety of ferns, including Japanese painted fern, fuzzy pale green lamb's ear, burgundy coral bells, and viburnum. In addition to its dark leafy greenery, viburnum produces small, aromatic balls of flowers. In the last section of this chapter, I explain how to create your own French cutting garden.

For those of you who have a garden, it's important to know that your flowers will last longer if you cut them in the early morning or evening. I never cut mine at midday, when the sun is at its hottest. The flowers are already stressed from all the heat and cutting them just adds to their anxiety, which will cause them to wilt faster. Hydrangea, hellebore, and lilac, in particular, can fade fast, so bring a bucket of water with you to the garden to hold the items you've just cut. If your flowers do wilt, I explain how you can refresh them in the Reviving and Hydrating Flowers section on page 184.

My second favorite source for florals is local flower farms and farmer's markets, and I encourage you to buy your flowers at these places, too. Increasingly, people are searching for sustainable flowers to support their farm-to-table ethos. Buying flowers locally helps reduce one's carbon footprint and guarantees the flowers will appear almost alive; they're so fresh. The climate you live in will determine what flowers your local farms can grow. Here in New England, I buy from several local flower farms, including one that raises a wide variety of gorgeously colored dahlias.

Since I own a floral business, I also buy flowers wholesale. Most big cities have wholesale flower markets, including Paris, which has Rungis with approximately 1,200 vendors selling every sort of plant material you can imagine, along with containers and garden decor. The flowers and greenery that I buy at my local wholesale market are the workhorses for my store and arrangements. The unusual varieties I use in my arrangements often come from my garden.

ABOVE AND OPPOSITE: *Peak-season roses and five-star-quality florals await discerning fleuristes at the wholesale flower market, Rungis.*

I do buy florals from abroad, particularly in winter when local blooms are not available. I also import flowers for wedding clients who often request specific blooms that may not be in season in New England. I tend to favor a handful of growers from Holland known for their high-quality blooms (often grown in hothouses) that arrive beautifully packed within twenty-four hours of being picked.

Another good source for flowers is your local florist. They will have a wide selection of seasonal flowers in various colors, sizes, and varieties, along with diverse foliage. Consider doing what the French do and bring your own vase to the florist. Then, you and one of the designers can pick out the appropriate blooms and greenery for the arrangement you'd like to make.

Specialty stores and supermarkets also carry flowers, and it's okay to buy them there. Whatever blooms

you do end up buying, make sure they have healthy green, not yellowing, leaves, are not losing petals, and appear perky, not limp.

Foraging can be an excellent way to supplement your plant materials, but just make sure to know any local, state, and federal laws about foraging in your area. What you find growing wild can add stunning texture and interest to your arrangement. I often take my dog, Obie, on walks into the woods behind my house to find unusual greenery, budding branches, and even patches of moss to use in my arrangements. However, it's also good to know which plants to avoid. This includes those that are endangered, rare, or poisonous or can cause irritation. (I suggest you wear gloves.) Also, the rule of thumb is to take only what you need from plants growing in abundance. And be sure not to damage the plant or the environment by picking.

How to Clean and Condition Your Plant Material

To extend the life of your flowers, it's vital to clean and condition them. At Les Fleurs, we immediately place all flowers and foliage in big buckets of room temperature water (cold and hot will shock them) after bringing them into the shop. We also put nutrients into the water. If you've bought flowers from a florist, they likely gave you a small packet of "flower food." This powdery white mix contains sugar that helps nourish the flowers and an acid and dried bleach, which slows the formation of bacteria in the water. Do add this mixture to your vase. If you don't have any flower food, you can make your own by mixing distilled white vinegar with sugar and bleach. I've included a recipe for you on page 184 under How to Make Flower Food.

Once all the plant material is in its special water, we use clean floral shears to snip off the bottom portion of the stems at an angle. This diagonal cut enables more water to enter the stem than if it were cut straight and keeps the blooms and foliage hydrated, thus preventing premature wilting. Make sure any flowers you bring home sit in room-temperature water with flower food for at least one hour. The process of transporting and cutting them has shocked them, and a rest in a nutrient-rich bath helps revive them.

For certain flowers, such as tulips, we remove any leaves that would be submerged in water, since the bacteria they carry will shorten the life of your arrangement. That's because a flower's leaves, not its bloom, are the first to drink up the water and nutrients. Finally, we arrange all the florals by type and color in glass containers and place them on our flower bar, just like the shops do in Paris, so visitors can see and enjoy the fragrance of our offerings.

Helpful Tools and Materials

As a professional florist, I regularly work with lots of tools and materials. However, you can start with a basic collection of items, including things you might have around your home. Below are the tools and materials I work with most, along with an explanation of when to use them. We sell most of the items at Les Fleurs. You also can find them online or in most garden centers.

PREPPING INSTRUMENTS AND ITEMS

APRON AND GARDEN GLOVES · Because I tend to be a "messy" designer, I started to wear an apron many years ago. It's long and made of black linen just like the one I used to wear in Paris. It protects my clothes by offering me a convenient spot to wipe the dirt and plant debris off my hands while I work. Gloves are also a big must when tackling most tasks in or around the shop. They help protect your hands when molding chicken wire (see the Supports section on page 71), placing flowering plants in containers, and working with thorny or prickly plant materials, such as roses and blackberry branches. While garden gloves come in a variety of materials, my favorite ones are from Showa Atlas and made of nylon and rubber. They are extremely lightweight and durable (see Helpful Sources, page 187) and I have several pairs around my store and one in my car in case I'm suddenly inspired to forage.

FLORAL SCISSORS · High-quality snips are my number one tool as a florist. I use them all day long to cut through stems when trimming and cleaning flowers and making my arrangements. While it's tempting to use household shears, the blades are simply too dull to tackle the job and will likely squash, not cut, the stems. For lighter stems, I love the Joyce Chen flower scissors, which are super sharp, lightweight, and have a comfortable plastic covering around the handles. For thicker stems, I recommend heavy-duty metal scissors, which are my workhorse scissors and even can cut wire.

SECATEURS (PRUNING SHEARS) · With a spring handle, these floral clippers help snap through tough stems and flowering branches. You also can use

Seventy-seven

Geum Urbanum
Common Avent   *Potandora Polygyria*

Chrysosplenium Alternifolium
Alternate leaved Golden Saxifrage
Tecandora Digynia
Stancombe

1
Water avens
Geum rivale
April 1848
...ds, riversides and damp banks

2
Wood avens or Herb Bennet
Geum urbanum
Woods and waysides

3
Alternate-leaved golden saxifrage
Chrysosplenium alternifolium
Stancombe
Scarce by shady stream-sides

Class 12th Order 5th Icosandria Polygynia

Rosa canina Dog Rose

Dog rose
Rosa canina
Hedges, scrub, open woods

them to cut chicken wire, which I explain below in the Supports section. I love the ash wood–handled ones with forged stainless-steel blades that we sell in our shop.

RIBBON SCISSORS · If you plan to make an abundance of hand-tied bouquets, which make lovely gifts, it's helpful to have a good pair of ribbon scissors to cut the silk and satin ties that will adorn them. The ones we use at Les Fleurs are Italian, and to make sure my staff knows to use them only for cutting ribbon, we tied a little ribbon around one handle. To find out where to buy them go to Helpful Sources on page 187.

SUPPORTS

FLOWER FROGS · These flat discs with spikes or small cages come in different shapes and sizes, as well as materials. They're often made of metal and meant to sit on the bottom of a vase holding the various stems that are stuck into them. I have trays of vintage flower frogs in various locations throughout my home. Some are used to display little photos and notes; others are waiting to be used for florals. You can secure flower frogs with the waterproof floral sticky clay as described on page 72 under Securing Items. If an arrangement is on the larger size, I usually use a flower frog in conjunction with chicken wire, which I talk about below. You might already have flower frogs at home. If not, you can find new ones at any garden center and lovely vintage varieties at local flea markets and antiques shops.

CHICKEN WIRE · This flexible mesh is essential for keeping my flowers in place and I often use it in conjunction with a flower frog inside my container. Chicken wire is available in different mesh sizes, and I like the green coated version best, since it won't rust and dirty your water. Also, coated chicken wire is more comfortable to bend and form than uncoated wire and the green version blends in with flower stems.

GREEN FLORAL TAPE (ALSO CALLED POT TAPE) · This thin, green tape is what I use to keep the chicken wire from popping out of my container. I simply place a strip across the center of the vase, trimming it about a half-inch down the side. This strip keeps the chicken wire nestled in the container. Once your arrangement is complete, the flowers and greenery will hide the tape and chicken wire. If you don't have any chicken wire or frogs, you can make a grid with floral tape across the top of your vase. This works best for arrangements that need minimal support.

FLORAL FOAM AND ECO-FRIENDLY ALTERNATIVES · On very rare occasions, I use floral foam, which I mention because so many florists use it. OASIS is one of the best-known brands and, thus, what many people say when referring to floral foam. Made of resins, this lightweight chemical substrate comes in various sizes and shapes, including bricks, rings, cylinders, balls, and cones. To use it, you cut whatever size piece you need to fit snuggly in your container and then soak the floral foam in water until it's saturated. The advantage of floral foam over other supports is that you can insert your stems at whatever angle you want, which is particularly useful for specific floral designs. The water in the foam helps hydrate your blooms and the resins slow down the growth of bacteria. The downside of floral foam is that it's contributing to the world's microplastic problem. As it breaks down, the tiny pieces enter the ocean and bodies of freshwater, ultimately sickening the creatures that ingest it. As a result, I seldom use it.

An environmentally friendly alternative to floral foam is a product called Sideau from the Netherlands-based company Agra Wool International. Made from spun volcanic rock fibers and a sugar-based binding agent, Sideau can be cut like floral foam and soaked in water. Sideau also can be reused. Another option is the Oshun Pouch from New Age Floral, a company in Sudbury, Massachusetts, not far from Les Fleurs. These biodegradable pillows contain coconut shell fibers that expand when the pouch is soaked in water to offer a "stabilizing hydration mechanic with superior insertion hold." See the Helpful Sources section on page 187 to find out where to buy both of these environmentally friendly items online.

SECURING ITEMS

COTTON AND JUTE TWINE · Both string types are helpful when tying bouquets and making garlands.

GREENING PINS (ALSO CALLED U-PINS OR FLORIST PINS OR FLORAL PINS) · These metal pins resemble tiny, square croquet wickets and come in different sizes. I find the two-inch size the most useful, particularly when securing, say, patches of moss to the base of an arrangement. In a pinch, you can bend a large paperclip into the same shape.

PIPE CLEANERS · I use long, green, fuzzy-coated pipe cleaners to secure the stems of hand-tied bouquets before wrapping them. The ones I buy are approximately twelve inches long.

RUBBER BANDS · Elastics are also helpful for keeping hand-tied bouquet stems together, once you've added the final piece of plant material. You likely have plenty of rubber bands at home.

WATERPROOF FLORAL STICKY CLAY · Sold in spools or as bricks, this clay can be molded into nuggets to adhere flower frog bases to vases.

WIRE ON A SPOOL · Wire is important for wrapping together cuts of greenery when making wreaths and wreath-like table arrangements, such as for a column candle. I use the green papered wire to secure sprays to stairwells and doorways, since the green paper exterior blends into the greenery. You can buy green paper wire in pre-cut lengths, which is handy when attaching a floral cluster to a bouquet or, say, pine cones to a wreath or garland.

EMBELLISHMENTS

FLORAL PAPERS, TISSUE, AND CELLOPHANE · Sturdy floral paper, such as brown craft paper and colorful floral tissues, will beautifully finish a hand-tied bouquet, just like you'd see in Paris. At Les Fleurs, we use brown baker's paper and a tissue bearing our logo that my mother picked out, not realizing it was the one I'd also chosen. We use the tissue for smaller arrangements and place the baker's paper inside of a piece of clear cellophane to wrap our hand-tied bouquets, which we tie with our signature custom-made Les Fleurs ribbon.

RIBBONS · Satin, grosgrain, and other ribbons are an essential final flourish to a French-style, hand-tied bouquet.

Creating Your Own French Cutting Garden

One of my favorite things to do at home is to grow flowers. I cherish being in my garden and seeing the beauty unfold in every bud and bloom. It's truly a labor of love.

I started gardening in my late twenties when I moved from the city to the suburbs. I formally announced to myself one day that as a florist, I really should have some type of garden where I could grow different sorts of flowers like the ones I remembered my grandmother growing. So, I got to work and planted as many bulbs and plants as would fit in my little plot, choosing everything based on when it would bloom, its durability, and ease of care. Then, *voilà*. With the arrival of spring came the first blooms.

At first, I didn't have the heart to pick any of the flowers. Those first pink and white hellebore of the season, followed by bright tulips and yellow daffodils, looked just so stunning after a long winter. So, I left everything in the beds. Eventually, however, I started cutting the flowers. I initially snipped only a few blooms and always in the back, hoping no one, meaning me, would notice they were gone. As time went on, my desire to cut more flowers to incorporate into my floral designs outweighed my concerns about leaving them in my garden.

Having my own garden enabled me to grow flowers and foliage not usually sold, like creeping clematis

and coral bells. And even though I have a slightly larger garden than the one I started with, I can't possibly grow all the florals I use in my shop. As much as I would love to, I'd have to buy more land and either quit my job and garden full-time or hire an entire garden crew to help cultivate the number of blooms I use. Since neither of those scenarios is an option, I am simply happy to have a little French cutting garden to supplement my designs. You can do the same thing. You can grow plants, shrubs, and florals in a relatively small space—even just in containers.

Since the most well-planned garden unfolds with the passing seasons—meaning just as one plant nears blooming, another one has unfurled its buds—you'll want to plant flowers that bloom in the spring, summer, and fall. Although I tend to grow all perennials, which come up every year, annuals are great for green thumbs who want particular flowers in their gardens and arrangements. If you plant flowers that need full sun, be sure they're in areas that get enough light each day. The same holds true for shade-loving plants; place them in the cool, dim areas of your garden. (Or don't plant them at all, if you have no shade.)

Below are the flowers, greenery, and herbs I grow in my own New England garden, along with select descriptions of my favorite seasonal flowers. Please note, there is no category for Winter Florals and Foliage because nothing blooms during these snowy months. Plant what works for you, based on the climate in which you live, the amount of space you have, available sun and/or shade, and what you adore.

SPRING FLORALS & FOLIAGE

bleeding heart · double daffodils · flowering branches · grape hyacinth
hellebore · hyacinth · lady's mantle · lilac · lily of the valley
peonies · roses · solomon's seal · spirea · tulips

BLEEDING HEART

Add these beauties to a shady part of your garden for delicate flowers shaped like tiny bleeding hearts. I always grow the white variety because they look so enchanting trailing from a centerpiece.

GRAPE HYACINTH
Muscari armeniacum

These smaller, more delicate cousins of regular hyacinth are at the top of my list of what I love to grow in spring. I plant them in late fall and they start sprouting in early spring, which is a joy after a long New England winter. I like to arrange them clustered in small cordial glasses.

HELLEBORE

Usually one of the first flowers to bloom in the garden, hellebore comes in a wide range of colors and has petite blooms that complement larger flowers in almost any arrangement. Grow them in groups to enjoy in your garden and as cuttings.

HYACINTH

When ordering spring bulbs, I always add a few hyacinths to my order. I like to plant them on the edges of my flower beds and in containers on my patio to view up close. Since hyacinths have shorter stems, I use them in petite bouquets and vases around my home.

LADY'S MANTLE

With its scalloped, roundish green leaves and tiny chartreuse late-spring/early summer flowers, lady's mantle makes great borders and ground cover. It loves shade and spreads like crazy, so don't overplant. It adds a bouncy frill to bouquets.

LILY OF THE VALLEY

One of the most fragrant blooming plants, lily of the valley has tiny, white bell-shaped flowers that add elegance to any arrangement. I plant them under the trees on the side of my home and use them in our shop for bridal events. They're also essential for making the *Fête du Muguet* arrangement (see page 170).

PEONIES

It's worth growing peonies, even for the few weeks they bloom in spring. Their big, showy blooms stand out in any garden or arrangement. I grow a variety of them, including tree peonies, which are woody shrubs with huge fragrant blooms that can measure up to ten inches in diameter.

ROSES

You can grow roses in garden plots, as well as pots. Just make sure they're in a sunny spot that receives at least six hours of sunlight daily. They like well-drained soil and need plenty of water. Deadhead spent blooms once a week to encourage new growth. Roses by nature are fragile and fleeting—they should last three to five days after cutting, provided you recut and change their water daily.

TULIPS

Plant tulip bulbs well before the first frost (in late summer or early fall) for beautiful spring blooms. Look for perennial varieties such as emperor and triumph tulips and one of my favorites, double 'Angelique' tulips, which have peony-like flower heads.

SUMMER FLORALS & FOLIAGE

astilbe · clematis · delphinium · foxglove · french lavender · garden roses · hydrangea · japanese anemones · lamb's ear · lisianthus · rudbeckia · sunflowers · sweet pea · wild raspberry vines · zinnias

ASTILBE

Available in shades of pink, red, and white, astilbe has glossy fernlike foliage and feathery flowers; I add it to my wedding designs because it adds a soft, willowy touch. The most common type is the hybrid variety, which blooms in late spring to early summer and prefers shade.

CLEMATIS

These climbing blooms make a lovely addition to a cutting garden. Plant clematis near a wall, trellis, or obelisk and let its vines ramble their way up to the top. Once they bloom, use them to add a whimsical texture to floral arrangements.

DELPHINIUM

While these come in many colors, the ones I grow are deep purple, light blue, and white. Their tall spikes of color pop in arrangements and feed hummingbirds when I don't cut them.

FOXGLOVE

The foxglove is a biennial, which means blossoms grow from seed the following season. It produces stunning tubular-shaped blooms in all sorts of colors. Plant enough to enjoy cuttings in your arrangements, but leave enough flower heads for reseeding.

FRENCH LAVENDER

One of my favorite plants to grow is French lavender—I am transported to Provence every time I catch its scent. It has lovely silvery-green foliage and fragrant dusty purple blooms. Cut it back after the first bloom in early summer and it will give you a second budding in late August.

HYDRANGEA

While hydrangea comes in various styles and colors, the ivory lacecap hydrangea I grow is a hardy plant that blooms all summer long, starting off creamy white and becoming pale pink. The flowers' lacy tops make them a delicate and refined addition to arrangements. My limelight hydrangea produces huge, lime-green blooms that pair beautifully in bouquets with some white and yellow flowers.

LISIANTHUS

I have a soft spot in my heart for the pale apricot version of lisianthus, which has smooth ruffled edges. I plant them in early spring for summer harvest.

SUNFLOWERS

Nothing says "summer" like a field of sunflowers. They remind me of Provence, where they grow in fields that look like a sea of yellow. I try to plant a few here and there in my garden but prefer some new colored breeds like 'Rouge Royale' (aka 'Moulin Rouge') with its burgundy hue.

SWEET PEA

With its colorful wispy blooms, twisting leafy stems, and honey-sweet scent, sweet pea is one of my favorite early summer florals and adds a delicate feminine touch to any arrangement. I also like to gather a large cluster of sweet peas and place them in an heirloom container, like a silver teapot.

FALL FLORALS & FOLIAGE

*coral bells · dahlias · grasses, including bunny tail, millet, and sea oats
herbs · Japanese painted fern · ninebark · pear tree · rosehip
scabiosa · sedum · smokebush*

CORAL BELLS
Heuchera

There are many varieties of coral bells, which have patterned, wavy, or ruffled leaves in colors ranging from celery green to almost black. The spring and early summer flowers, also known as Heuchera, attract hummingbirds and butterflies and come in hues of coral, red, white, or pink, depending upon the variety.

GRASSES

Fall grasses are an exciting way to add movement to your floral designs. While there are many kinds to choose from, my favorites include millet, sea oats, and bunny tail, which, as the name indicates, has fluffy ivory tips reminiscent of the white cottontails of rabbits. I like to add fresh or dried bunny tail grass to arrangements for a touch of softness. You can dry all of these grasses by hanging them upside down in a dark area for several weeks. Once dried, arrange them in one or two favorite containers to enjoy after your garden has faded.

HERBS
Basil, Mint, Purple Sage, Rosemary

I often add herbs to my arrangements, especially the smaller ones. Aside from giving bouquets an authentic French touch, herbs add a pleasing aroma. Cuttings of cool mint and grassy basil enhance summer posies, while sprigs of rosemary and sage add a woodsy warmth to autumnal bouquets.

JAPANESE PAINTED FERN

This silvery green fern with purple-red midribs keeps its lustrous patina through fall as most other ferns begin to wilt and brown. Since these types of ferns do like the shade, make sure to plant them in a protected part of your garden out of full sun.

NINEBARK

I love my large ninebark shrub for its tall coppery-bronze leafy limbs. These branches add substance and grandness to my floral designs. If you choose to grow ninebark, find an area with plenty of space, because it can grow up to ten feet tall.

PEAR TREE

I treasure the 'Chanticleer' pear tree in my garden, not for its fruit (the pears are small and bitter), but for its white spring blossoms and striking foliage, which goes from shiny green in spring and summer to golden orange and even purplish red come fall.

SEDUM

Sedum has thick, succulent pale green leaves and waxy flower heads in lime, pink, and other colors, making it a beautiful addition to any garden. The low-growing variety nicely edges paths and rock gardens, while the upright ones are best for cutting. A bonus is that sedum also attracts bees, thus aiding in cross-pollination.

SMOKEBUSH

Smokebush, with its deep crimson hue, is perfect for autumnal bouquets. It makes an ideal complement to the brighter jewel tones often used during this time of year.

french floral

—

RECIPES

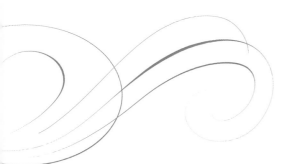

Who doesn't love flowers? With their rich and muted colors and sweet fragrance, flowers can set a mood or send a message, often more effectively than words. A special arrangement can evoke a sense of joy, serenity, and even gratitude. Flowers make a home feel more beautiful, and their fleeting existence makes them that much more special.

In the floral recipes that follow, you'll find detailed directions for creating arrangements that feel balanced both visually and physically. Please note, under the ingredient list, when possible, I have given the flower's trademarked name that the breeder or nursery titled it, such as Oregon-based Heirloom Rose's pale-apricot-colored 'Moonlight in Paris' rose I used in the *Célébration de Roses* (Rose Celebration) on page 98. If you're not able to find the trademarked name flower, simply substitute a similar color bloom. Below are some general guidelines for creating any arrangement, particularly for the compote-style ones I love to design.

After choosing the proper container for this style arrangement, I like to put it on a lazy Susan. I can spin my creation around while I design, seeing it from every angle. Next, I add the supports of a frog and chicken wire, secured with tape. I prepare the frog by attaching a piece of sticky clay tape to the frog's bottom. Then I secure the frog to the bottom of the compote by pushing it down and gently turning the frog to get the sticky clay tape to "lock" into place. Once the system is secure, I cut my coated chicken wire, usually to two times the size of the container. Then I shape the wire into a round or oval form and place it into the container over the frog with the cut portion on the bottom. I prevent the chicken wire from rising up by placing a strip of floral tape over the center of the container and about a half-inch down each side. Finally,

I fill the container with room temperature water, since most flowers prefer that, and add flower food.

Next, I cut and prepare all my plant materials, cutting the stems and removing any dead or extraneous leaves or petals. Then I organize everything by variety and color in small bundles in my workspace. The French call this *mise en place*, a term for having all your ingredients measured, cut, peeled, and sliced before you start cooking.

I usually start at the base of the arrangement using various greens, including any herbs or foraged foliage from my garden. Here, I love to mix foliage, such as lemon leaves and cuts of Viburnum, rather than just using one type of green. Strive to use your greens to cover the entire container, hiding your mechanics and creating a good base. Try placing a few additional stems at an angle, allowing several to cascade over the edge of the container to create movement and interest. Your greens will dictate the shape of your arrangement. Therefore, I love to take a step back and look at the foliage before adding my flowers.

Next, I add my large, linear flowers, like butterfly bush blooms, placing them at alternating heights to add interest and structure to the arrangement.

You can achieve this by cutting your flowers into different lengths. Then I add my circular flowers, like roses, making sure to turn the blooms outward to face the viewer. Nestle a few together with at least one of them tucked more tightly into the arrangement. This will add structure. It also prevents your design from looking too uniform and evokes a more garden-style look. Be sure to add some flowers toward the base of your arrangement. This adds movement and, if your creation is for a dining table, offers visual interest for seated guests.

Now, it's time to add pockets of daintier material like sweet peas, foxglove, and astilbe. Let them float high in the arrangement. When your creation feels almost complete, consider pruning it to give it some breathing room. This means removing extraneous flowers and foliage to give the arrangement an airy, loose look.

Finally, I tuck in a few focal or face flowers, which are the stars of the show. I love to use large extravagant stems like peonies, dahlias, or garden roses. These eye-catching elements anchor the arrangement and prevent it from looking too busy or over foraged. Give everything a spritz of water to keep the flowers fresh and, *voilà. C'est fini.*

DINING ROOM ARRANGEMENTS

One of my favorite activities is setting my dining room table for a family gathering or dinner for friends. It's a chance to pull out my favorite linens, crockery, glasses, and candles to create a beautiful table that's even more striking with florals. The season often dictates the colors I use. However, I sometimes like to choose unconventional colors to create a mood, such as aubergine linens and Dijon mustard–colored tapers on a Thanksgiving table. The look is rich and inviting, yet pleasantly unpredictable. No matter what arrangement you choose to put on your table, you'll want it low enough so that guests can see over it. You also want to avoid using fragrant flowers like freesia, which could overwhelm the food. Finally, make sure there are flowers at eye level, since everyone will be seated for most of the meal.

Set against a background of spring wisteria, this outdoor dining table supports an aged terra-cotta compote artfully filled with a romantic mix of garden roses, soft pink peonies, ranunculus, bleeding heart, and frothy white spirea.

LA VIE EST BELLE

life is beautiful

Spring

SEASON

CONTAINER

Table

LOCATION

Once the weather becomes warm enough, I love to host friends for a meal in my garden. It's a great excuse to pull out my mismatched vintage pieces (received as hand-me-downs and found in France) and set a table with layers of different patterns and colors. This rose arrangement brings back fond childhood memories of snipping a rosebud or two (maybe three!) from my maternal grandmother's cutting garden.

ingredients

One 8-inch-wide low cement bowl or urn

One 3-inch flower frog

Floral putty

One 12-inch piece coated chicken wire

Floral tape

7 stems of short foraged or purchased greenery (I used lamb's ear, sage leaves, and sprigs of herbs)

3 stems grape ivy, snipped from an ivy plant

5 pale peach garden roses

5 pale pink garden roses

5 ivory-taupe garden roses

5 small pale pink bud roses or majolica spray roses

3 white Japanese anemones

3 crabapple branches

method

1. Prepare your container by fastening the flower frog to the bottom with floral putty. Shape the coated chicken wire into an oval. Insert the chicken wire into the container over the flower frog. Secure the wire with floral tape. Fill the container with room temperature water and add flower food.

2. Insert your greenery and ivy through the chicken wire into the frog evenly around the container. This will create the structure for your arrangement.

3. Begin adding in the roses, layering them amid the greenery and clustering the paler shades together to give you that just-picked-from-the-garden look. If your table is on the longer side, extend several of the roses from either side of the container. A good rule of thumb is to give every bloom its own space and don't be afraid to move your flowers around until you are satisfied with the final version.

4. Tuck the anemones and crabapple branches around the bottom area.

CLOCHES DE PÂQUES

easter bells

Spring

SEASON

CONTAINER

Table

LOCATION

In France, instead of the Easter bunny bringing sweet treats, *les cloche volantes* or "flying bells," bring them. According to legend, all French church bells stop ringing on the Thursday before Easter to fly to Rome to mourn Jesus's crucifixion. But the bells don't return home empty. Instead, they carry colored eggs and chocolates to drop in gardens across France for children, who eagerly listen for their returning sound on Easter morning. This colorful, airy tablescape is a festive way to celebrate the holiday *à la Française*. If you have some bells, do scatter them on the table.

ingredients

7 or 9 petite, assorted bud vases and cordial glasses

Two 6-inch-high clear, glass cloches on saucers or French Limoges dessert plates

3 bells, if using

20 stems grape hyacinth (*Muscari armeniacum*)

3 pale yellow garden roses

7 peachy-coral ranunculus

5 purple hyacinth

2 purple anemone

2 pale pink tulips

6 stems deep pink sweet pea

2 large pink garden roses

2 purple clematis

3 fern stems

12 feverfew buds plucked from a large sprig

Assorted fruit: 6 clementines, 9 kumquats, 2 lemons

method

1. Arrange the small vases and cordial glasses down the center of the table, setting each holder slightly off center, to create a vignette. Once the holders are in place, fill each one with room temperature water and flower food. Place the cloches toward the ends of the table and add the bells, if using. Stand back to see how everything looks and move the various elements around until you are satisfied.

2. Place 15 stems of the grape hyacinth in a cordial glass near the cloche on the left side of the table. Then, working left to right, place 1 pale yellow garden rose in the first front vase, 1 in the back middle, and the remaining yellow rose on the right front area of the table. Next, add your ranunculus and purple hyacinth to the various holders. Not every vase will hold the same flowers.

3. Add the purple anemones to two holders between the cloches. Add the pink tulips to two other holders. Lastly, add the remaining 5 stems of grape hyacinth and the stems of sweet pea to whatever six vases could use some color. Consider adding 2 stems of grape hyacinth and 2 stems of sweet pea to a single holder to add rhythm.

4. To anchor the collection of vessels, you'll use the 2 large pink garden roses as your "face flowers." Place the roses in two vases that are far apart so they don't compete. Place 1 stem of clematis next to each rose to add a little bounce to those vases.

5. Add the fern stems to three vases that could use extra foliage. Then, scatter the feverfew buds down the table, place 3 clementines inside each cloche, and add the remaining fruit throughout your tablescape.

CÉLÉBRATION DE ROSES

rose celebration

Early Summer		*Table*
SEASON	CONTAINER	LOCATION

Most of the garden roses that I use for my wedding work arrive from Grace Rose Farm in California. Their roses are exquisitely fresh and come in a variety of styles and colors. The farm takes great care when packing the flowers and ships all over the United States. On those rare occasions when I have some leftover wedding roses, I'll arrange them in a large stoneware crock, as you can see in this arrangement I composed during strawberry season. The ruby-red fruit beautifully complements the soft colors of the roses, which I highlight by not adding any foliage to the arrangement. Simplicity at its best. If you don't have a stoneware crock, feel free to use any similar-size container.

ingredients

One 15-inch piece coated chicken wire

One 10-inch-wide vintage stoneware crock

Floral tape

7 light gold 'Butterscotch' garden roses

12 mauve 'Koko Loko' garden roses

12 taupe 'Stephen Rulo' garden roses

12 pale apricot 'Moonlight in Paris' garden roses

7 light pink 'Jubilee Celebration' garden roses

method

1. Shape your coated chicken wire into a ball and insert it into your container. Secure the wire with floral tape. Fill the container with room temperature water and add flower food.

2. Trim 5 of your light gold roses to the height of the container and place in the wire evenly around the container. Keep the other 2 roses a bit longer and position them so that they drape over the side of the container.

3. Trim the mauve roses in varying stem lengths to create movement in your design and avoid a ball-shaped arrangement. The goal here is to have that just-picked-from-the-garden look. Since the roses have the same rounded shape and size, it's important to vary stem length. For a display with multi-shaped blooms in various sizes you wouldn't need to do this.

4. Next, add your taupe and pale apricot roses, trimming the stems in varying lengths so that a few dangle over the container's edge for interest. Since the colors of these roses complement each other, cluster several of each color together in different places to lead the eye in and around the bouquet.

5. Finally, add the light pink roses, interspersing them between the other roses, filling in the areas that have gaps to create an abundant whole.

Butterscotch

Stephen Rulo

Moonli

Koko Loko

Jubilee Celebration

Paris

CLÉMENTINES

clementines

Summer

———

SEASON

CONTAINER

Table

———

LOCATION

If you need a quick centerpiece for your table, this is the answer. I love filling this
unique vintage ironstone container with whatever blooms are growing in my garden.
Don't worry if you don't have this type of holder; you easily can recreate it. Simply stack
three different-sized bowls—a 10-inch-wide bowl, a 9-inch-wide bowl, and a 7-inch-wide
one—with a small cup set in the center of each of the bottom two bowls to elevate the
bowl resting on top of it. Then, to secure your stems, use clear tape to create a grid pattern
on the bottom two bowls and place a 2-inch-wide flower frog (secured to the bowl's
bottom with floral putty) in the top bowl. Feel free to use any combination of flowers
and herbs you want to create your own version of this French-style arrangement.

ingredients

One 3-tiered vintage
ironstone flower frog vessel,
   or
one 10-inch-wide bowl,
one 9-inch-wide bowl, and
one 7-inch-wide bowl, stacked

10 white love-in-a-mist
(Nigella damascena)

20 peachy coral ranunculus

method

1. Fill the ironstone vessel (or stacked bowls) with room temperature
   water and add flower food.

2. Trim some of the love-in-a-mist stems so that they are longer than
   the ones you're going to put in the middle and top tiers. Evenly
   disperse the blooms around the entire bottom section. Continue
   adding the nigella in this same manner to the remaining two levels,
   trimming the stems accordingly.

3. Cut the ranunculus stems to various lengths to create movement
   throughout the arrangement and place them throughout the three
   tiers. Once you've put all the flowers in the three tiers, stand back
   and see if you need to further trim any blooms or rearrange them to
   fill any obvious gaps.

POTS DE YAOURT DE FLEURS

flower yogurt cups

Fall		*Table*
SEASON	CONTAINER	LOCATION

When setting your next fall table, whether it's for dinner with friends or Thanksgiving, think outside the standard orange, rust, and golden palette. Instead, reach for an unexpected but seasonal mix of warm creamy tones, set off with touches of dusty rose and burgundy, as with these florals tucked into French stoneware yogurt cups and pots I picked up in France. This floral "runner" interspersed with tiny white pumpkins and squash is a refreshing change from the large single centerpiece that typically graces a dining table.

ingredients

Three 13-inch pieces coated chicken wire

Three 8-inch pieces coated chicken wire

Three 5-inch pieces coated chicken wire

Three 6½-inch-wide, 3½-inch-high French stoneware yogurt cups or pots

Three 4-inch-wide, 3-inch-high French stoneware yogurt cups or pots

Three 2½-inch-wide, 3-inch-high French stoneware yogurt cups or pots

Two 1-inch-wide and 8-inch-high stoneware bottles

5 pear tree branches

7 leaves deep burgundy 'Palace Purple' Heuchera

7 leaves light green 'Shimmer' Heuchera

7 lavender-beige 'Amnesia' roses

5 pinkish cream 'Blizzard' dahlias

3 stems sedum

8 stems spirea

5 stems seeded eucalyptus

7 dusty rose 'Jowey Winnie' dahlias

3 off-white David Austin 'Tranquility' garden roses

2 purple hyacinth bean vines

2 beige 'Mini *Café au Lait*' dahlias

Twine

Dinnerware, flatware, and napkins

2 wheat sheaths per napkin

7 to 9 small white pumpkins

3 'Black Futsu' squash

2 honeynut squash

1 vintage brown transferware platter (holding cheeses and fruit)

- continued -

method

1. Shape each piece of coated chicken wire into a ball and insert them into the containers, with the largest in the largest containers and so on. Fill the containers and stoneware bottles with room temperature water and add flower food.

2. Arrange the holders on your table by placing larger pots near smaller ones to add interest. Place one stoneware bottle to the left of the table's center and the other bottle to the center's right.

3. Trim and add 1 pear branch to each of the three large containers. Next, add 1 burgundy Heuchera leaf to each vessel's left side and 1 light green Heuchera leaf to the right side of each. Add 2 lavender-beige roses to each pot, placing the roses diagonally across from each other. Nestle 1 pinkish cream dahlia into each holder, followed by 1 stem of sedum. Lastly, tuck into each 1 spirea stem and 1 stem seeded eucalyptus.

4. Working with your three medium containers, place the remaining 2 pinkish cream dahlias in two of the three pots. Add 1 dusty rose dahlia and 1 off-white garden rose to all three vessels. Add 2 light green Heuchera leaves to one pot, 2 burgundy leaves to the second pot, and a burgundy and light green Heuchera leaf to the third pot. Add 1 seeded eucalyptus stem to two of the medium holders.

5. Working with your three small containers, place the last burgundy Heuchera leaf in one pot and then the last light green Heuchera leaf in another. Add the final lavender-beige rose to one vessel. Then, add 2 dusty rose dahlias to the pot containing no Heuchera leaves; add 1 dusty rose dahlia to each of the other two holders. Finally, add 1 spirea stem to two of the small containers.

6. Place 1 pear branch, 1 purple hyacinth bean vine, and 1 small beige dahlia in each stoneware bottle.

7. Set your table. Tie a piece of twine around each rolled napkin and tuck in 2 wheat sheaths. Intersperse the pumpkins and squash down the table, along with the final 3 spirea stems.

MANTELPIECE ARRANGEMENTS

Regardless of the season, it's nice to highlight an
unexpected area of your home, such as a mantel, with
a bouquet. Flowers on this ledge can add an element of
surprise when entering a room, and mantels are often
overlooked when decorating. Your vase doesn't have to be
too large—a pretty urn or collection of small holders will do.
If your mantel is in a dining room and you're hosting a dinner,
you may want to skip putting florals on the table to avoid
everything looking overwrought. Or keep the table florals
(or just greenery) extremely simple.

A potpourri of white porcelain and cut-glass holders in assorted
shapes and sizes cradle a bounty of spring blooms atop this Paris apartment's
mantel. The central arrangement—lush with pale pink roses, peach-apricot
lisianthus, and white star-shaped bellflowers—grounds the tableau
(see page 120 for recipe), while smaller side florals add softness and fluidity.

BOUCHÉE DE FLEURS

a bite of flowers

Spring

SEASON

CONTAINER

Mantel

LOCATION

Not long ago, I visited my friend's home in Normandy. Upon walking into her salon, I was struck by how artfully she had arranged her collection of ironstone gravy boats, tureens, and platters on her cottage mantel. It was so beautiful and inspiring that I headed into her garden and gathered florals to create this little gravy boat arrangement that's one of five you can make to dress your mantel. Don't worry if you don't have a collection of gravy boats—you can use whatever other smallish containers you have in your cupboards, such as creamers, sugar pots, and pottery pitchers.

ingredients

Coated chicken wire
or clear tape

5 ironstone vintage gravy boats
or other small containers

8 sprigs foraged or purchased
greenery, such as lilac leaves,
mint, and flowering oregano

6 snippings of purple
'Amazing Havana' clematis

4 white garden roses

3 stems 'Million Stars' astrantia

5 light pink garden roses

4 pale pink 'Mother's
Choice' peonies

5 stems lavender 'Butterfly
Blue' scabiosa

method

1. You can add a small ball of chicken wire to each vessel or make a grid over each one using clear tape in a crisscross pattern. Place the gravy boats (or other small containers) on the mantel, moving them around until you find an appealing composition. Fill each holder with room temperature water and add some flower food.

2. Starting on the left side of the mantel, place 1 sprig of greenery in your first vessel, leaning it to the left. Place another sprig in the next container, leaning it to the right. Continue adding the remaining sprigs in this manner to give your overall creation a balanced look.

3. Trim each clematis stem and add 1 each to four of your five containers. Add the remaining 2 clematis to the fifth holder. Next, trim the white garden roses and add 1 each to two of your five holders and 2 to a third holder. Add 2 of the astrantia to the two containers without white roses and the third astrantia to whatever third holder you'd like. We want each composition to look different. We're going for a loose garden feel.

4. Trim and add the light pink garden roses, either to each container or add 1 light pink rose to a container, and double up in two of the containers. Trim and add the peonies in the same manner. Add 3 scabiosa to one holder and the remaining 2 to whatever two holders you'd like. Stand back and rearrange the blooms until you have a pleasing design.

FLEURS DU JARDIN

garden flowers

Spring

SEASON

CONTAINER

Mantel

LOCATION

There are so many fun and creative ways to dress a mantel, including placing an arrangement on just one end, as I do here. The vintage urn I use is made of stone and comes from a *brocante* in the French countryside. Although I haven't used that many blooms for this arrangement, it has a lush abundance and romantic looseness, which complements the aged, gilded mirror behind it.

ingredients

One 6-inch-wide stone urn or similar container

One 3-inch flower frog

Floral putty

4 stems foraged or purchased foliage

3 pale pink 'Mother's Choice' peonies

5 salmon-peach 'Wild Look' roses

2 deep pink garden (or regular) roses

3 cream-colored 'Romantic Pepita' spray roses

2 snippings of purple 'Amazing Havana' clematis

2 lime-green 'Winterbells' hellebore

3 light pink lisianthus

2 pale pink *Allium nectaroscordum*

3 magenta-colored pansies

method

1. Prepare your urn by fastening the flower frog to the bottom with floral putty. Fill the urn with room temperature water and add flower food.

2. Secure the first stem of foliage into the frog at an angle so that it sweeps up to the right side of the urn. Add the second stem so that it sweeps down to the left, thus leading the eye from the upper right to bottom left. Repeat these angles with the remaining 2 stems of foliage to add contrast, symmetry, structure, and height to your arrangement.

3. Trim your first peony on the shorter side and place it in the middle portion of the urn to ground the arrangement. This is your focal flower. Trim the stems of the remaining 2 peonies and add them along your greenery's upper and lower lines. Next, add the salmon-peach roses and large deep pink roses to both sides of the urn, playing off the peonies and adding height and width to the arrangement.

4. Trim the cream-colored spray roses and nestle 2 to the left of your focal flower (peony) and the third over the urn's right edge. Snip the stems of clematis and hellebore and arrange them so that they almost fall out of the urn.

5. Finally, add the lisianthus and allium along the lines of the greenery, keeping the stems long to draw the eye upward. Finish by tucking in the pansies, their rich hue beautifully offsetting the soft pastels used throughout.

PRINTEMPS À PARIS

springtime in paris

Spring

SEASON

CONTAINER

Mantel

LOCATION

I created this romantic pink and white arrangement to showcase the rouge marble mantel of this Haussmann-style apartment in Paris. Constructed in the nineteenth century, these buildings have limestone facades, wrought-iron wraparound balconies, and opulent interiors featuring chevron parquet floors, high ceilings, intricate plasterwork, and majestic marble fireplaces topped with gilded mirrors, like the one you see here. To me, these are the prettiest buildings in Paris.

ingredients

One 10-inch piece
coated chicken wire

One 10-inch-wide,
5-inch-high oval ironstone
compote urn

Floral tape

3 stems mock orange

3 stems star jasmine
(*Trachelospermum jasminoides*)

3 stems white English stock

3 light pink astilbe

6 light pink
'Sweet Escimo' roses

5 light peach-apricot lisianthus

2 white bellflower campanula

2 white love-in-a-mist
(*Nigella damascena*)

method

1. Shape your coated chicken wire into an oval and insert it into your container. Secure the wire with floral tape. Fill the container with room temperature water and add flower food.

2. Arrange the mock orange and star jasmine evenly around the compote base so that they cascade over the rim.

3. Trim 1 stock stem and position it to run diagonally to the right side of your container to elongate your centerpiece. Add another stock sweeping up to the container's top left portion to add movement. Add the third stock to the container's back right side to add volume.

4. Trim 1 astilbe and add it to the lower-left portion of the arrangement. Add the second stem to the top right and tuck the third into the back of the arrangement. Your composition's structure will now be in place and ready for your tighter, more rounded flowers.

5. Trim 3 roses relatively short. Add 1 to the center lower portion of the arrangement and cluster the other 2 toward the left side. Keep the stems of the other 3 roses longer, about the same length as the stock, and nestle them into gaps on the arrangement's right side, following the linear pattern of the flowers already in place.

6. Now, trim some of the lisianthus flowers shorter and place them so they hang slightly over the lip of the container. Keep the others longer and disperse them throughout the arrangement.

7. Cluster the bellflower campanula, your "face flowers," to the center-right of the arrangement to give your display a fuller look.

8. Add the love-in-a-mist to areas that could use softness and movement.

SIDEBOARD &
CREDENZA
ARRANGEMENTS

Whether your sideboard or credenza is in your hall,
dining room, or living room, its elongated surface can
hold a wide variety of floral arrangements in different
shapes and sizes. You can set one statement piece upon
it or adorn it with a more straightforward arrangement
to complement a collection of treasured items.

———————

An antique wooden sideboard in a private château in Provence provides the
perfect spot for this elegant spring medley of white peonies, snowy delphiniums,
and emerald olive branches in a vintage stone pedestal urn.

TULIPES EN JARDINIÈRE

tulips in a planter

Spring		*Sideboard*
SEASON	CONTAINER	LOCATION

If you're celebrating an important event and want a statement piece for an
entry table or sideboard, this is your arrangement. I love the aged patina of this
vessel, along with its elongated shape, which lends itself to using different linear
branches and florals to give you that "just gathered" French country style.

ingredients

One 20-inch piece
coated chicken wire

One 12-inch-wide oval
vintage iron jardinière
or similar container

Floral tape

2 apple blossom branches

3 fern stems, any variety

2 stems Solomon's seal

4 stems pink bleeding heart

6 stems lavender lilacs

3 snippings of deep pink
'Inspiration' clematis

7 purple 'Double Price'
peony tulips

6 white 'Clearwater' tulips

5 lily of the valley sprigs

2 pale pink hellebore

method

1. Shape your coated chicken wire into an oval and insert it into your
   container. Secure the wire with floral tape. Fill the container with
   room temperature water and add flower food.

2. Slit the bottom of each apple blossom branch (for better water
   absorption). Secure 1 branch in the container leaning to the left and
   the other leaning to the right. This will let your eye float throughout
   the arrangement.

3. Next, tuck in your ferns and Solomon's seal along the lines of your
   apple blossom branches, hiding the chicken wire as you go.

4. Add your bleeding heart, lilac stems, and clematis, positioning them
   to cascade over the sides of your container to soften the edges and
   add lightness and bounce.

5. Next, trim your purple peony tulips and tuck them toward the
   bottom of the arrangement to anchor it. Keep your white tulips
   relatively long to float them freely in the upper portion of the
   arrangement to add height and dimension.

6. Lastly, tuck in the delicate sprigs of lily of the valley and hellebore
   where you see fit.

PLUMES FLORALES

flower quills

Summer

SEASON

CONTAINER

Sideboard

LOCATION

One of my favorite pastimes is to visit vintage shops and flea markets to discover interesting objects to fill with pretty blooms. I often look for different styles and sizes of clear glass ink bottles and small cordial glasses and have amassed a treasured collection. Here, I've clustered several of these holders together with a glass cloche to create an easy yet artful arrangement. You also can scatter these holders around your home to fill those spots that could use a little floral boost.

ingredients

12 clear glass vintage ink bottles and cordial glasses in varying sizes

One 4-inch-wide glass cloche with a bottom saucer or other cloche and saucer

9 dahlias in different colors and sizes

2 deep purple lisianthus

3 white or light pink foxgloves or snapdragons

1 to 2 handfuls foraged moss for your cloche (be sure to keep moss moist by spritzing with water)

7 stems foraged or purchased greenery, such as fern, weigela leaves, and fresh mint

1 purple coneflower (*Echinacea purpurea*)

5 sprigs lavender

method

1. Arrange the ink bottles, cordial glasses, and cloche on your sideboard to create a pleasing composition. Make sure no same-size holders are standing next to one another to give your arrangement room to breathe.

2. Fill a small watering can with room temperature water and add flower food. Fill each glass holder with the water.

3. Place dahlia blooms in nine different holders, putting the larger dahlia blooms in the larger holders.

4. Place both lisianthus blooms where you feel they'll contrast nicely with your dahlias. Add foxgloves to three of your taller holders.

5. Arrange your tufts of misted moss on the saucer of the cloche. Tuck 2 stems of greenery into the moss, trimming as necessary so they'll fit under the glass dome. Nestle the stem of the coneflower into the moss. The moist moss will act as a water source for the coneflower and greenery. Place the cloche over the moss, greenery, and bloom.

6. Finally, add the sprigs of lavender, cut into different lengths, to whatever holders need a boost, along with the remaining greenery. Stand back and rearrange your stems and greenery as necessary to create a textured, exciting vignette.

ÉCLAT DES DAHLIAS

burst of dahlias

Late Summer Early Fall		*Sideboard*
SEASON	CONTAINER	LOCATION

I made this arrangement for a September workshop at an estate not far from Les Fleurs that could have been in France. Set on lush grounds, the estate has beautiful gardens reminiscent of those I've seen in the South of France. When the students arrived, they walked under an arch of dahlias and roses to enter a candlelit greenhouse with place settings holding all the items they'd need to make their creations, including masses of locally grown dahlias, containers, tools, and, of course, glasses of wine. It was an enchanting evening and a reminder of why I love to offer workshops in France and beyond.

ingredients

One 11-inch-wide, 6½-inch-high terracotta compote-style container (if there is a drainage hole in the container's bottom, plug with floral putty or a trimmed cork)

One 3-inch flower frog

Floral putty

One 20-inch piece coated chicken wire

Floral tape

5 stems lemon leaf

3 stems Italian *Ruscus*

3 stems native fern

3 peach-colored 'Orange Wonder' snapdragons

3 salmon-colored 'Apricot Beauty' foxgloves

2 blush-colored dinnerplate *'Cafe au Lait'* dahlias

5 coral 'Snoho Doris' dahlias

3 white-edged orange *'À La Mode'* dahlias

3 pinky-peach 'Peaches and Cream' dahlias

3 apricot 'Cornel Bronze' dahlias

3 pale peach 'Juliet' garden roses

3 coral-colored roses

3 orange 'Free Spirit' roses

3 peach 'Shimmer' roses

2 stems coral spray roses

7 coral strawflowers

3 stems native New England orange-colored berries or hypericum berries

- continued -

method

1. Prepare your container by fastening the flower frog to the bottom with floral putty. Shape your coated chicken wire into a ball. Insert the chicken wire into your container over the flower frog. Secure the wire with floral tape. Fill the container with room temperature water and add flower food.

2. Trim 3 lemon leaf stems and place them on either side of the compote. Cut the remaining 2 slightly shorter and add toward the center of the container to cover your mechanics. Next, arrange your Ruscus leaves and fern to fall naturally on both sides of your arrangement, flanking the lemon leaves.

3. Add your snapdragons and foxgloves to the upper and lower corners of the arrangement to add height and length.

4. Trim your *Café au Lait* dahlias and place 1 in the center of the arrangement to create a focal point. Turn the container around and place the second dahlia in the center of the back. Then, using all your different shades of dahlias, mix them throughout the design, trimming them at varying lengths. This will help achieve the loose feel you want.

5. Next, add the different shades of roses to your design. I like to cluster my roses together, cutting one a little shorter than the others. Also, tucking a few of them close to your dahlias will add fullness and depth.

6. Finally, tuck in your strawflowers and berry stems, which are your "dancer" flowers and will add a dainty feel to the arrangement.

COULEURS D'AUTOMNE

autumn colors

Fall

SEASON

CONTAINER

Sideboard

LOCATION

Fall in New England has a magical quality, especially in my garden.
As the weather turns cooler, the foliage and florals take on a richer, more exciting
look: the sedum now has a burgundy hue, the ferns and greenery have taken on a
golden patina, and the dahlias and zinnias are competing for best in show.
Seeing all these deepening colors and textures is inspiring as a designer. In fact,
I often have to remind my clients that some of the most striking arrangements
take advantage of autumn's unexpected treasures—the leafy branches,
berry-rich foliage, and ferns that could be growing in their own backyards.

ingredients

One 7-inch-wide, 7-inch-high
vintage glass compote

One 3-inch flower frog

Floral putty

One 6-inch piece
coated chicken wire

Floral tape

6 branches ninebark
(3 green and 3 dark burgundy)

2 branches Japanese maple

2 branches Amur maple

2 branches brown
copper beech leaves

Three 8-inch snippings of
clematis vine without flowers

3 leaves from a deep burgundy
'Palace Purple' Heuchera

3 branches linden arrowwood
(*Viburnum dilatatum*)

3 deep yellow
'Hamari Gold' dahlias

3 deep apricot
'*Crème de Cognac*' dahlias

3 salmon-bronze
'Sierra Glow' dahlias

5 dusty rose
'Jowey Winnie' dahlias

7 'Swizzle Scarlet and
Yellow' zinnias

- continued -

method

1. Prepare your container by fastening the flower frog to the bottom with floral putty. Shape your coated chicken wire into a ball. Insert the chicken wire into your container over the flower frog. Secure the wire with floral tape. Fill the container with room temperature water and add flower food.

2. Trim and add the ninebark to the left and right sides of the compote. This will act as your guide when adding the other greenery.

3. Next, start adding both varieties of maple branches, the copper beech branches and clematis vines, positioning them so they fall naturally on the right and left sides of your arrangement. The goal is to use the greenery to create a subtle U-shape structure for the flowers.

4. Tuck the Heuchera leaves and branches of linden arrowwood along the compote's edge to create texture.

5. Trim your deep yellow dahlias to different lengths and place the shortest in the center of the arrangement. Place the second one to the left and the third one toward the upper right. Cluster the deep apricot and salmon-bronze dahlias toward the front section of the composition to anchor it. These dahlias are your "face flowers" and will help keep the arrangement from visually floating away or looking like a vase of vegetation.

6. Nestle the dusty rose dahlias near the larger dahlias. Then, place 1 zinnia in the arrangement's lower left area and 1 in the upper right. Add the remaining zinnias to any dark sections that could use a pop of color.

RÊVE D'AUTOMNE

autumn dream

Fall	*container*	*Sideboard*
SEASON	CONTAINER	LOCATION

I created this large-scale floral display for a client who was hosting a festive fall event at her home. Even though this arrangement looks grand, it's quite simple to create. The framework consists of vegetation that I cut from my property, but you easily can substitute whatever similar greenery grows near you. What adds to the wow factor of this masterpiece is the bounty of apricot, gold, cream, and salmon-pink garden roses that play off the dark, moody foliage.

ingredients

One 14-inch-wide, 9½-inch-high dark gray iron footed urn

One 10-inch-wide round low glass bowl insert

One 3-inch flower frog

Floral putty

One 20-inch piece coated chicken wire

Floral tape

3 pear tree branches

3 spider flower (*Grevillea*) greenery stems

3 branches Banksia integrifolia

3 branches brown copper beech leaves

5 stems spirea

5 stems seeded eucalyptus

3 stems spiral eucalyptus

5 to 7 blades foraged grasses, such as millet, sorghum, and oat

3 bracken ferns (which patina to a beautiful golden color in the fall)

7 large rust-colored chrysanthemums

5 taupe 'Purity' garden roses

3 pale peach 'Juliet' garden roses

2 peachy cream 'Princess Maya' garden roses

7 butterscotch-colored 'Caramel Antike' garden roses

5 stems ivory lacecap hydrangea (which turn a soft crimson in the fall)

3 stems dusty rose 'Flamingo Feather' celosia

- continued -

method

1. Prepare your container by nestling the glass bowl inside. I use moss from my woods to secure the bowl, so there is no movement when designing. Fasten the flower frog to the bottom of the glass bowl with floral putty. Shape your coated chicken wire into a ball. Insert the chicken wire into your glass bowl over the flower frog. Secure the wire with floral tape. Fill the container with room temperature water and add flower food.

2. Place your tallest branches of pear tree, spider flower greenery, and Banksia integrifolia into the chicken wire and flower frog in an asymmetrical fashion to give a natural garden feel to the arrangement. Next, add your smaller greenery, starting with the branches of copper beech leaves, spirea, and the different varieties of eucalyptus. Trim the foliage to follow the line you created with your taller branches. This will give the piece a fuller look.

3. Trim the grasses and add them to the outer edges of your composition so that they cascade over the sides. The idea is to create a willowy arrangement inspired by an autumnal garden. Add the ferns, trimming them enough so that they bow over the rim of the urn. You now have the structure for your display.

4. Trim your rust-colored chrysanthemums to varying lengths and add them to the composition, starting from the top left and working your way down to the middle, since most people look at floral displays from left to right. Add in the different colored roses, placing most of them in the left and front areas of the arrangement and a few toward the upper and lower right sections. Next, add the hydrangea along the bottom front area to soften the container's edge. Finally, add your wispy "dancer" celosia to the lower right, upper center, and left areas. Stand back and adjust any flowers and foliage as necessary.

KITCHEN
ARRANGEMENTS

Given how much time we spend in our kitchens,
there's nothing like a gorgeous arrangement to make you
smile inside every time you make your coffee, have lunch,
fix dinner, or simply pass through this space. While an island
is a natural spot to place a bouquet, the counter area is a
lovely alternative. In France, where kitchens tend to be
smaller and used less for gatherings and more for cooking,
you'll often see fresh flowers on the counter.

A French white ceramic water pitcher makes a perfect container for this pink and
lavender bouquet brimming with showy pink peonies, pink roses, double-petal
tulips, and blush anemones (see page 151 for recipe). Set on a café table outside the
kitchen of this home in Provence, the arrangement will soon head back inside to
add a colorful breath of spring to *la cuisine*.

CUEILLETTE DU JARDIN

garden harvest

Fall
SEASON

CONTAINER

Kitchen
LOCATION

Autumn is when I start to bring the outside in. My garden is beginning to slow down, and I pick the last of the flowers and foliage before they fade away. Here, I pair a few statement flowers with loads of contrasting foliage from my backyard, and I encourage you to do the same with the foliage near you, substituting as necessary. The stoneware crock I found in Normandy offers a rustic contrast to the luxurious plant materials.

ingredients

One 15-inch piece coated chicken wire

One 10-inch-wide vintage stoneware crock or similar container

Floral tape

12 curly willow branches

12 stems various eucalyptus

3 olive or rosemary branches

3 stems spider flower (Grevillea) greenery stems

3 stems yellow 'Safari Goldstrike' conebush (Leucadendron)

3 pink Sylvia Protea or large pink hydrangea blooms

7 light pink roses

7 pink-green ranunculus

3 apricot-colored lisianthus

3 stems dusty miller

1 medium bunch privet berries

5 deep crimson scabiosa

method

1. Shape your coated chicken wire into a ball and insert it into your container. Secure the wire with floral tape. Fill the container with room temperature water and add flower food.

2. Cut the curly willow branches so that they are at least two times the height of the container. Arrange them evenly throughout the container to create the arrangement's structure.

3. Next, add your eucalyptus stems, dispersing them evenly throughout the arrangement in a circular pattern. Place the olive branches, spider flower greenery, and conebush stems among the willow branches and eucalyptus, arching these items left to right to complement the overall structure and soften the height.

4. Add the Sylvia Protea, the "face flowers," toward the bottom area to ground the arrangement. Then add your medium-size cylindrical flowers, which are the roses, ranunculus, and lisianthus. Trim the stems at varying lengths and place these flowers throughout the arrangement.

5. Nestle the smaller and more delicate dusty miller and privet berries around the base of the container to add softness and fill any holes that may show your mechanics (chicken wire).

6. Finally, add your scabiosa blooms, or "dancer" flowers, to add movement throughout your bouquet.

FRAMBOISES ET CRÈME

raspberries and cream

SEASON

Spring

CONTAINER

LOCATION

Table

For a floral workshop in Provence, I scooped up these fragrant pink florals at the Marché aux Fleurs, a famous open-air market in Nice overflowing with flowers and locally grown produce. The handcrafted, cream-glazed holder comes from a pottery shop in the charming village of Moissac-Bellevue.

ingredients

One 15-inch piece
coated chicken wire

One 5-inch-wide, 10-inch-high
white ceramic water pitcher

5 stems purple lilacs

3 stems white flowering spirea

3 snippings deep pink clematis

5 pink 'Monsieur Jules
Elie' peonies

5 pink 'Sarah
Bernhardt' peonies

3 blush and deep magenta
'Ballarena De Saval' peonies

5 light pink 'Sweet
Escimo' roses

3 pink double tulips

5 blush anemones

3 stems Queen Anne's lace

method

1. Shape your coated chicken wire into a ball and insert it into your container. Fill the container with room temperature water and add flower food.

2. With the pitcher's handle on your right, arrange most of the lilacs and spirea stems around the pitcher's base, allowing several to cascade over the pitcher's rim. Add the remaining stems so that they sweep up toward the right side of the container.

3. With the structure of your arrangement in place, trim and add your clematis along the foliage lines.

4. Add the peonies, starting with one in the lower center area of the container. Add the rest along the foliage lines. Add 1 rose to the lower left side of the arrangement, 1 in the upper center area, and 1 in the upper right area. Turn the pitcher around and add 1 rose to the left side of the arrangement and the last rose to the upper center area. Turn the pitcher back around with the handle on the right.

5. Add the double tulips in the lower left and center-left portion of the arrangement. Nestle 1 anemone next to each rose.

6. Finally, place 1 Queen Anne's lace stem in the lower left side of the container, reaching out. Place another stem toward the upper left and the third sweeping toward the right. Adjust any flowers that have gotten blocked.

CONTE DE FLEURS

flower fairy tale

Summertime is all about enjoying the outdoors as much as possible, particularly when entertaining friends and family. During these warmer months, my garden bursts with blooms that I love to use to create rustic arrangements like this one—my way of saying, "Welcome to our home," without the fuss of a complicated floral design. In addition to the gorgeous tall delphiniums in shades of blue and lavender, I added some wispy garden flowers like nigella and tweedia in the same color palette. A tall zinc bucket, typical of the vintage galvanized flower buckets found all over France, adds to the arrangement's informality. Set it on a pretty table outside, as you see here, or on a kitchen island loaded with hors d'oeuvres.

ingredients

One 15-inch piece coated chicken wire

One 12-inch-wide zinc French flower bucket with a plastic liner

Floral tape

12 dark blue 'Elatum Blue Star' delphiniums

12 lavender 'Aurora' delphiniums

12 light blue belladonna delphiniums

20 light blue tweedia (*Oxypetalum coeruleum*)

10 white love-in-a-mist (*Nigella damascena*)

10 blue love-in-a-mist (*Nigella damascena*)

method

1. Shape your coated chicken wire into an oval and insert it into the top portion of your container. Secure the wire with floral tape. Fill the container with room temperature water and add flower food.

2. Trim your dark blue delphiniums so that each one is twice the height of the container. Place 1 stem in the container's center. Trim 2 stems slightly shorter than the center stem and place 1 on either side of the center bloom. Rotate your container and repeat this process. Add the rest of your dark blue delphiniums, trimming them appropriately so that they form a tall, elongated shape.

3. Using the same method as above, trim and add your lavender delphiniums, placing them close to the dark blue delphiniums. Doing this will give the arrangement an *en masse* look. Again, keep turning your container so you can place flowers on all sides.

4. Add the light blue delphinium, whose thin shape will add a wispy, airy look to the arrangement, followed by the tweedia. Because these flowers are shorter-stemmed and have a slight bend to them, I add them to the base of the container. Having them spill over the edge creates movement and interest.

5. Finally, tuck in the white and blue love-in-a-mist where you see gaps. I usually grab both colors and add them together to the arrangement to offset the tall, bushy delphiniums.

SIDE TABLE
ARRANGEMENTS

There's no quicker way to add a stylish touch to your living room or salon than with a pretty little arrangement on a coffee table or side table. It can wake up a sleepy space and lend a pleasing pop of freshness. Likewise, you can place these bouquets on a bedside table or in a powder room.

———————

An ornate vintage French glass and gold vessel holds a simple rose posy, which adds a graceful and fragrant touch to this Parisienne guestroom.

BELLES TULIPES

beautiful tulips

Spring

SEASON

CONTAINER

Side Table

LOCATION

There are some arrangements that I return to again and again, including this one. Having always been charmed by the Dutch master tulip paintings of the seventeenth and eighteenth centuries, I have recreated that lush, abundant look here with masses of Dutch tulips spilling out of a glass compote. Since tulips are the first sign of spring, especially after a long, gray New England winter, this arrangement is a welcome ray of sunshine.

ingredients

One 6-inch-wide glass compote

One 3-inch flower frog

Floral putty

One 10-inch piece
coated chicken wire

Floral tape

12 pink lily-flowered 'Crown
of Dynasty' tulips

10 pink frilly-edged
'Bell Song' tulips

3 stems pale pink hyacinth

1 branch flowering white quince

10 white peony tulips

15 white and pink tulips

2 pale pink hellebore

method

1. Prepare your compote by fastening the flower frog to the bottom with floral putty. Shape your coated chicken wire into a ball. Place the chicken wire over the flower frog in your container. Secure the wire with floral tape. Fill the container with room temperature water and add flower food.

2. Start creating the shape of your arrangement by placing 5 pink lily-flowered tulips into the frog around the base of the compote. Next, add 5 of the pink frilly-edged tulips, in the same manner, followed by the 3 stems of hyacinth. Finish by placing the single stem of flowering white quince on the left or right side, whichever looks more pleasing.

3. Now is the time to add all 10 of the white peony tulips, clustering a few together in the arrangement and equally dispersing the rest in a balanced manner. It's okay if these flowers and the remaining ones are not in the frog. The chicken wire will support them.

4. Next, add all 15 of the white and pink tulips, making sure to turn your arrangement around to ensure that the flowers are nicely dispersed vertically and horizontally around your arrangement. You are building in more texture and variety.

5. For this final step, you're going to add the remaining flowers, cutting the stems at different lengths to add interest. Begin by adding the remaining 7 pink lily-flowered tulips, the remaining 5 pink frilly-edged tulips, and the pale pink hellebore. Rearrange your flowers as necessary to fill any gaps and create a pleasing whole.

BELLES PETITES TULIPES

beautiful petite tulips

Spring
SEASON

CONTAINER

Side Table
LOCATION

Here is a mini version of the same sort of arrangement.
Because it's so tiny, you don't need any supports.

ingredients

One 4-inch-wide thin vase

3 pale pink tulips

3 white and pink tulips

3 white peony tulips

2 pink frilly-edged
'Bell Song' tulips

2 stems pale yellow hyacinth

method

1. Fill your vase with room temperature water and add flower food.

2. Gather 1 of each variety of flower in your hand. Keep adding all the flowers until you have a balanced bouquet. Hold it next to your container and cut the stems so that the flowers will just mound over the top of your container. Drop the bouquet into the vase and adjust any stems as necessary until you have a nice rounded shape.

LE LILAS

the lilac

Spring

———

SEASON

CONTAINER

Side Table

———

LOCATION

One of my dreams is to own a French country home with a massive garden where I can grow all my favorite flowers, including rich purple lilacs. I love how their sweet fragrance fills the air, especially when you bring them inside and put them in a vase. For this arrangement, I chose a plain, ivory-colored ceramic milk pitcher to showcase the intricate flower clusters. A tip when working with lilacs—since their woody stems quickly form bacteria in water, let them soak for 20 minutes or so in a bucket of water mixed with a few drops of bleach. Then, when you're ready to arrange them, use shears to make cuts up the stems for water absorption. Finally, change the arrangement's water daily.

ingredients

1 ivory-colored ceramic milk pitcher

One 3-inch flower frog

Floral putty

7 purple lilac branches, each with multiple flower clusters

method

1. Prepare your pitcher by fastening the flower frog to the bottom with floral putty. Fill the container with room temperature water and add flower food.

2. Place 1 lilac branch on the left side of the pitcher near the handle so that it cascades over the edge. Place another branch on the pitcher's right side near the spout to drape right. Place 3 lilac branches in the back section of the pitcher, leaning toward the right. Cut the remaining 2 lilac branches shorter than the back ones and tuck them into the center front. Adjust the branches as necessary to create a pleasing composition.

LE CYGNE

the swan

Summer

SEASON

Container

CONTAINER

Side Table

LOCATION

This graceful arrangement takes its name from a crystal swan salt cellar I bought at my favorite Parisian antiques market, the Marché aux Puces de la Porte de Vanves. That same day, I also found this vintage glass ice bucket and knew it would make a perfect vase for this simple gather-and-drop bouquet, which needs no mechanics (i.e., flower frog or chicken wire). Together, the floral-filled swan and ice bucket make a pretty pair, especially when set on a side table overlooking the streets of Paris, as they do here.

ingredients

One 5-inch-wide vintage glass ice bucket

7 pieces foraged or purchased foliage, such as lilac greens, star jasmine vine, and herbs, like mint sprigs

2 blush-colored 'Bella Donna' peonies

3 stems lavender English stock

3 pale pink 'Mondial' roses

method

1. Fill the container with room temperature water and add flower food.

2. Strip away any greenery from the foliage and blooms that will sit below the container's water line. Working with one piece of foliage at a time, place a stem in your dominant hand and keep adding more stems to create a bouquet of greenery that will serve as your foundation. You don't need to use the tapping method and twist the bundle as you go, as when making a hand-tied bouquet, because you're aiming for a loose, wildflower look. Trim all your foliage stems to the same length, approximately double the height of your container.

3. Place each peony in your bouquet of greenery so they'll face out when put in the vase. Next, add the stock, 1 on the left side of the bouquet, the other just off-center to the right, and the third on the lower right. This placement avoids creating a ball-shaped bouquet. Finally, tuck in the roses and drop the arrangement into the ice bucket. Adjust the flowers and greenery as necessary, lifting them up slightly to give them more breathing room.

GIFT & SPECIALTY ARRANGEMENTS

Whenever I am invited to someone's house for dinner or another such event, I do what the French do and bring florals. Of course, being a florist, I always have gorgeous flowers on hand. Usually, I bring a hand-tied bouquet; aside from its being simply beautiful, all the host needs to do is place the arrangement in a vase. Other arrangements that follow can be given as gifts or placed in unexpected areas of the home, such as a raised landing in front of windows, on a staircase, outside on a patio, or on the edge of a piano. Your space will let you know what should go where.

———

Bouquets of cream, pink, and lime-green florals dress up the steps of this château in Provence. The iconic white stoneware Parisienne milk jugs, repurposed as vases, come from Manufacture de Digoin, which handcrafts stoneware pieces for the kitchen and garden in the Burgundy region known as the "Ceramic Valley."

FÊTE DU MUGUET

lily of the valley festival

Spring

SEASON

CONTAINER

Gift

LOCATION

The first of May is a double holiday in France. It's May Day, known as Fête du Muguet (Lily of the Valley Festival), and Labor Day, or Fête du Travail. Most public and private businesses close and friends and family traditionally exchange bouquets of lily of the valley to bring good luck, celebrate friendship, and commemorate the return of spring. Following the French tradition, you can give loved ones a compote arrangement, like the one I've made here with lily of the valley from my garden, or a small posy wrapped with twine. Whichever one you choose, it's a thoughtful way to show your affection.

ingredients

One 10-inch piece coated chicken wire

One 10-inch-wide, 5-inch-high white oval compote or other similar-size container

Floral tape

80 to 100 stems lily of the valley, half of them with leaves

method

1. Shape the coated chicken wire into an oval and insert it into the container. Secure the wire with floral tape. Fill the container with room temperature water and add flower food.

2. Insert the lily of the valley leaves through the chicken wire evenly around the container. This will create the structure for your arrangement. Then add the flowers in clusters evenly throughout to create a puffy, full arrangement.

FÊTE DES MÈRES

mother's day

Spring

SEASON

CONTAINER

Gift

LOCATION

The French celebrate Mother's Day in late May by giving every *maman* a beautiful wrapped floral bouquet. I always marvel at the gorgeous hand-tied bouquets the French *fleuristes* display outside their shops on this holiday, enticing all the passersby. Every shop has its own bouquet style, and the one below includes many of my favorite spring flowers, all chosen for their different textures, colors, and meanings.

ingredients

5 stems spirea

3 stems viburnum foliage

3 stems Solomon's seal

Three 10-inch-long snippings from a grape ivy (I have a grape ivy in the shop just for cutting)

5 snippings of purple 'Amazing Havana' clematis vine

3 lavender larkspurs

3 lavender snapdragons

3 white love-in-a-mist (*Nigella damascena*)

2 blue love-in-a-mist (*Nigella damascena*)

3 stems green-tinged 'Charlotte Pink' hydrangea

3 lime-green 'Winterbells' hellebore

2 white 'Million Stars' Astrantia

3 blue *Triteleia* brodiaea

3 beige 'Sahara' roses

3 pink 'Mondial' roses

3 sprigs lavender spray roses

5 light pink butterfly ranunculus

3 stems 'Delft Blue' hyacinth

3 leggy 10-inch-long lavender and purple pansies (mine are from my outdoor pot)

1 long green pipe cleaner, or 1 elastic band

1 ribbon

Craft paper

- continued -

method

1. Begin by organizing each variety of flower and foliage in small piles based on the order in the ingredient list. To help form your bouquet's spiral shape, I start with the greenery to form the base and then add the flowers using the tapping method. This method involves creating the bouquet in your left hand and using your right to add foliage and flowers. You'll begin by taking your first stem and slanting it so you can tap the top of the vegetation or bloom on your shoulder. This method ensures you'll add the stem to your bouquet at the correct angle. With each stem you add, turn your bouquet a quarter twist and add another stem using the same method. Be sure to hold the greenery and flowers somewhat loosely to create a relaxed garden-style bouquet instead of a tight, bunched-up one.

2. Using the tap method, place 1 spirea stem loosely in your left hand, and with your right hand tap the tip of the next spirea stem on your shoulder and place it over the first stem. Turn the 2 crossed stems a quarter of a twist and add the third spirea stem. Continue building the bouquet in this manner in order of the greenery listed until you have added the last snipping of clematis vine.

3. Start adding your flowers in the order they are listed, beginning with your lavender larkspur. Make sure you cut the flower stems at slightly different lengths before adding them; this is how French flower shops add bounce to their bouquets.

4. Once you've added the pansies, it's time to secure your bouquet. Wrap the pipe cleaner or elastic band tightly around the top portion of the stems and trim the bottoms to your desired length. Tie a pretty ribbon over the pipe cleaner or elastic and wrap in craft paper (see page 184) as they do in Paris!

PASTELS D'ÉTÉ

summer pastels

Summer

SEASON

CONTAINER

Gift

LOCATION

Toward the end of June, my New England garden abounds with voluptuous fragrant peonies and sorbet-colored roses from the famous British rose breeder David C. H. Austin. To highlight the flamboyant lushness of the peonies and roses, I offset them with delicate blooms and place the whole arrangement in an earthy stone pot versus a fancy crystal one.

ingredients

One 15-inch piece
coated chicken wire

One 8-inch-wide, 6-inch-
high decorative stone pot
with a 6-inch-wide glass
cylinder vase liner

Floral tape

3 stems salvia foliage

3 stems ornamental
oregano foliage

3 stems mountain mint

3 stems black raspberry foliage

3 lavender butterfly
bush flower spikes

3 stems spirea

3 white David Austin
'Madame Hardy' roses

3 purple garden spray roses

3 deep pink astilbe

3 'Blushing Bride' protea

5 white 'Festiva
Maxima' peonies

3 blush-colored peonies

2 pink 'Sarah
Bernhardt' peonies

3 stems white lacecap
hydrangea

- continued -

method

1. Shape your coated chicken wire into a round and insert it into your glass cylinder vase liner inside the stone pot. Secure the wire with floral tape. Fill the container with room temperature water and add flower food.

2. Using the greenery to create the structure of your arrangement, place the salvia foliage on the right and left back sides of the container. Add the oregano foliage and mountain mint in the same manner, thus creating a back support area of greenery.

3. Add 1 stem of black raspberry foliage toward the right front of the container; add the other stems toward the back left. Nestle each butterfly bush spike near each black raspberry foliage stem. Tuck in the spirea so that 1 stem is on the arrangement's left, another near the center back, and the third on the right. Add 1 white David Austin rose to the lower center area of the arrangement. Turn the container around and place a second one in the same location. Turn the container back to face you and add the third white rose to the lower left area of the display.

4. Add the purple garden spray roses to the arrangement where you see gaps. Tuck 1 stem of astilbe in the upper left back portion of the arrangement, another stem in the lower left area, and the third stem toward the upper right side. Cluster the protea in the upper left portion of the arrangement.

5. Place half of the peonies in the arrangement's lower and upper center areas. These are your "face flowers." Turn the container around and similarly place the remaining half in the back of the arrangement. Turn the container back to face you and nestle the lacecap hydrangea in the container's lower right area and toward the back. Stand back and adjust any flowers and foliage as necessary to create a full and balanced composition.

LE BOUQUET DE FLEURS

floral bouquet

Late Summer

SEASON

Gift

CONTAINER

Gift

LOCATION

When I lived in Paris, I got used to shopping daily for my food, as the French do. After work, I would join the throngs of people ducking in and out of the *boucherie*, *boulangère*, *fromagère*, and other purveyors. People's bags brimmed with produce, long baguettes, and very often hand-tied floral bouquets. That's because the French consider flowers an essential ingredient in life. A bouquet like this one isn't just for special occasions—it's a way to add a touch of beauty and grace to your home on a regular basis.

ingredients

3 stems wild indigo
(*Baptisia australis*) foliage

3 stems African blue basil

Three 8-inch-long
snippings of grapevine

3 branches smoke bush

3 stems spirea

2 stems pennycress

2 soft orange 'Sierra
Glow' dahlias

3 white-edged orange
'À la Mode' dahlias

7 peach 'Apricot
Beauty' foxgloves

3 stems sedum

3 stems limelight hydrangea

3 burgundy snapdragons

3 light pink lisianthus

5 tufts 'Little Bunny'
fountain grass

3 mauve 'Jazzy Mix' zinnias

5 creamy salmon-colored
'Chamois' China asters

2 burgundy 'Love Lies
Bleeding' amaranthus

3 magenta 'Double Click
Bicolor Violet' cosmos

1 long green pipe cleaner,
or 1 elastic band

1 ribbon

Craft paper

- continued -

method

1. Begin by organizing each variety of flower and foliage in small piles based on the order in the ingredient list. To help form your bouquet's spiral shape, start with the greenery to form the base and then add the flowers using the tapping method. This method involves creating the bouquet in your left hand and using your right to add foliage and flowers. You'll begin by taking your first stem and slanting it so you can tap the top of the vegetation or bloom on your shoulder. This method ensures you'll add the stem to your bouquet at the correct angle. With each stem you add, turn your bouquet a quarter twist and add another stem using the same method. Be sure to hold the greenery and flowers somewhat loosely to create a relaxed garden-style bouquet instead of a tight, bunched-up one.

2. Using the tap method, place 1 wild indigo stem loosely in your left hand, and with your right hand tap the tip of the next wild indigo stem on your shoulder and place it over the first stem. Turn the 2 crossed stems a quarter of a twist and add the third wild indigo stem. Continue building the bouquet in this manner until you have added the last stem of pennycress.

3. Start adding your flowers in the order they are listed, beginning with your soft orange dahlias. Make sure you cut the flower stems at slightly different lengths before adding them; this is how French flower shops add bounce to their bouquets.

4. Once you've added the cosmos, it's time to secure your bouquet. Wrap the pipe cleaner or elastic band tightly around the top portion of the stems and trim the bottoms to your desired length. Tie a thick satin ribbon over the pipe cleaner or elastic and wrap in craft paper (see page 184).

HELPFUL FLORAL TIPS

HOW TO WRAP A HAND-TIED BOUQUET

Fold a large rectangle of craft or baker's paper almost in half at an angle to create two corner peaks, one larger than the other. Then, with the folded portion toward the stems, place the bouquet, which you already have tied with a luxurious ribbon, so that the blooms lie between the two corner peaks. Next, fold the left side of the paper over and around the flowers and secure with clear tape. Fold the right side over the bouquet and secure with tape. At the shop, we place a sticker on the swaddling and tie the paper portion just above the stems with more of our signature gray ribbon.

REVIVING AND HYDRATING FLOWERS

When certain flowers, like hydrangea, lilac, and hellebore, are cut, the plant tries to "heal" the wound by closing the stem. The result can be wilting. You can counteract this by having a bucket of cool water with you when clipping your flowers and immediately plunging the stems in the water. For hydrangea, a trick to making the flowers last longer is to make a short cut in the stem's center and then dip the cut stem in a chemical compound called aluminum potassium sulfate, which you'll find in the spice aisle. Cooks use the compound, sometimes labeled as alum, to keep pickles crisp, and when the stems of fast-wilting flowers, like hydrangea, are dipped in it, the alum encourages the stems to drink up more water. Another trick I use for extending the life of hydrangea and hellebore is to dunk the entire blossom head in a pot of cool water to freshen and revive it. For flowers like lilac and tulips, I immediately trim off the leaves, since they drink up the water first.

EXTENDING THE LIFE OF FLOWERS

Your flowers will last longer if you change the vase water daily, which removes any bacteria. With each water change, add flower food to nourish the blooms and further cut down on bacteria production. Recut flower and foliage stems every few days to help them absorb more water. For poppies, I have an additional step. When their stalks are first cut, they release a milky substance that shortens their lives. To prolong it, I burn the bottom portion of each stalk with a lighter, thus cauterizing the stem and preventing the milky residue from seeping out.

MANIPULATING FLOWERS

Most flower varieties are hardier than you think and can be touched without marring or browning their petals. Gardenias are an exception and shouldn't be touched. You can blow on roses to open the centers and even pick out petals from the center to open them up more. You also can remove a few petals from flowers, like ranunculus, if the petals are blocking the center.

HOW TO MAKE FLOWER FOOD

Measure out 1 quart of room temperature water and whisk in 1 tablespoon distilled white vinegar, 1 teaspoon superfine sugar, and 4 drops of bleach. Store mixture in a lidded container and add 1 tablespoon to a small vase, 2 tablespoons to a medium vase, and 3 tablespoons to a large holder.

The easy art of reflexing flowers, shown with this pale pink rose, gently pulls open the petals to create a showier, bigger bloom.

REFLEXING FLOWERS

You can pull back the petals of certain flowers through a method called reflexing. I use this to make certain flowers, such as roses, look bigger and more open. Start by removing any guard petals around the outside base of the rose. Then, working from the outside in, gently pull down each petal with your forefinger on the petal's front and your thumb on its back, stopping when the center petals become too stiff to pull down.

USING HOUSE PLANTS AND CONTAINER FLOWERS IN YOUR ARRANGEMENTS

When making arrangements, particularly smaller ones, I often turn to my houseplants and potted containers outside for inspiration. I love adding a few ferns and snips of ivy vines, such as jasmine vine or angel vine, to give my arrangements a unique twist. When I grow containers full of pansies during the warmer months, the tiny flowers tend to get leggy over time. So, I simply snip a few of these delicate blooms and add them to my bouquets for added interest.

HELPFUL SOURCES

Here are some of my favorite sources for garden items, flower arranging tools, embellishments and plant material in both in Paris and the United States.

PARIS

Containers and Embellishments

Alix D. Reynis
22 rue Jacob, 75006
alixdreynis.com
It's the beautiful, handmade porcelain pieces that I buy from this quaint shop in the heart of Saint-Germain des Près to use as containers for flowers. From sauce boats and vases to compotes and pitchers, these holders are simple yet refined.

Marché Saint-Pierre
2 Rue Charles Nodier, 75018
marchesaintpierre.com
The Marché Saint-Pierre store is next to the Basilique du Sacré-Coeur, a corner of Paris brimming with similar boutiques selling an enticing selection of beautiful buttons, ribbons, fabric, and other notions.

Ultramod
4 Rue de Choiseul, 75002
This enticing shop sells a sumptuous array of buttons, vintage ribbons, notions, and more, as it has since 1832.

Garden Accessories and Decor

Deyrolle
46 rue du Bac, 75007
deyrolle.com
Since 1831, this shop has specialized in taxidermy and entomology, available for viewing and buying (all creatures perished of natural causes and were donated by institutions like zoos and circuses). But those in the know beeline to the ground floor to stock up on the exquisitely crafted Le Prince Jardinier line of garden goods.

Marin Montagut
48 Rue Madame, 75006
www.marinmontagut.com
This store makes you want to scoop up everything you see, including the whimsical hand-painted plates, serving pieces, and garden-themed pillows, prints, and home décor, all courtesy of artist-owner Marin Montagut. He opened up his namesake shop on the left bank to showcase his talents, including his best-selling book *Timeless Paris*.

Fresh Flowers

Marché de Rungis
rungisinternational.com
I've been to many wholesale flower markets over the years for my shop, but no place has ever impressed me more than the Parisian flower market Rungis. Located just a short distance from Paris by car, it's one of the largest wholesale markets in the world. Rungis also offers public tours so you can witness the magnificence of its flowers firsthand.

OUTSIDE OF PARIS

Floral Supplies

Floral Genius
floralgenius.com
This company manufactures the flower frog and pin holders we use for most of our floral creations. These holders come in a wide range of shapes and sizes.

Jamali Garden
jamaligarden.com
Here you'll find an impressive selection of unique containers and décor often used in the floral trade but available for retail. They also carry other items, including candles, planters, and floral supplies.

- continued -

New Age Floral
newagefloral.com
This company sells several earth-friendly alternatives to floral foam.

Niwaki
niwaki.com
Here is your one-stop shop for all types of shears, scissors, and clippers, hand-crafted and made to last for generations.

Showa Atlas
showagroup.com
Showa Atlas are my go-to gloves when designing florals or working in my garden. They have a snug fit and are very comfortable. The style I buy is the Atlas® 300. I even keep a pair in my car for last-minute foraging.

Embellishments

May Arts Ribbon
mayarts.com
This company carries an enormous selection of ribbons in all sorts of materials, colors, patterns, and widths.

Silk & Willow
silkandwillow.com
This is where I buy botanically hand-dyed silk ribbons that I often use to tie my bridal bouquets. Available in an array of colors and textures, these ribbons will add a luxurious touch to any gift and floral creation.

Studio Carta
studiocartashop.com
My friend Angela Liguori opened this beautiful, sunlit atelier near Boston to showcase the exquisite custom-crafted ribbons, sewing products, papers, and writing accessories of her homeland, Italy.

Bulbs, Flowers, and Other Garden Sources

Adelman Peony Gardens
peonyparadise.com
I have a slight obsession with peonies and have over 30 different varieties in my garden. Most of the unique ones come from Adelman Peony Gardens. A good tip: Be sure to follow the company's planting and harvesting instructions, including letting your peonies get settled into their surroundings before harvesting.

Breck's
brecks.com
Since the company's founding in 1818, Breck's has been supplying growers with gorgeous varieties of bulbs straight from Holland. I especially love their unique types of daffodils and alliums.

David Austin Roses
davidaustinroses.com
When I decided to plant a few varieties of garden roses at my home, I looked no further than roses from David Austin, a notorious rose breeder whose roses are bred in Shropshire, England and grown in the United States. The roses have beautiful blooms and an outstanding fragrance. I purchase the bare root roses that the company ships in early spring.

Find Local Flower Farms
localflowers.org
When looking to purchase from local growers for in-season blooms, head to this site. It will list farms near you and the flowers they grow.

Floret
floretflowers.com
This Washington State family-run flower farm is a terrific source for flowers, specialty seeds, and tools. It also offers workshops and courses for those who want to grow, harvest, and even sell seasonal blooms. One of the founders, Erin Benzakein, also has written several flower and garden books.

Grace Rose Farm
gracerosefarm.com
Located in sunny California, this is one of the growers from whom we buy our garden roses. We use the cut stemmed roses for our wedding and event work—the farm ships the flowers overnight in an insulated box to ensure freshness.

Rose Story Farm
rosestoryfarm.com
This family-owned farm grows over 130 varieties of exceedingly fragrant heirloom garden roses.

ACKNOWLEDGMENTS

There are many people to whom I owe a big *merci beaucoup* for helping me create this book. It has taken almost three and a half years of photo shoots, Zoom calls, writing periods, and editing sessions to get this book to the finish line, and I am indebted to everyone who helped me get there. There were times when I worried that I wouldn't finish this project, but you helped bring it to fruition.

A special thanks to my incredibly talented Rizzoli editor, Sandy Gilbert, art director, Jan Derevjanik, and agent, Leslie Stoker, for your endless patience and guidance. You've held my hand every step of the way, always answering my questions and concerns with words of encouragement.

To Victoria Riccardi, my constant companion and co-writer, who was by my side for every part of this book. You were more than a support—you were a mentor who made this process worthwhile. You were my shining star through all of this. Thank you, my friend.

To my sweet, dear Kindra Clineff, who was the one who encouraged me to do this book many years ago. We had so much fun together, whether jumping on a plane to capture pretty photos of all my favorite Parisian spots or meeting in a field to shoot beautiful flower arrangements. These are the moments I will cherish. I miss you and wish you were here to see the final version of this book, but I know you are here in spirit.

A sincere thank you to Jody Clineff and Tim Preston, who, despite our mutual sorrow, helped Kindra live on in this book through her extraordinary photos. I have no words to express my gratitude.

To Anne Soulier, my wonderful French photographer friend, for always showing up at a moment's notice to capture the beauty of France in all your photos. *Merci beaucoup.*

To Abby Matses, Jamie Jamison, and my niece Paige Clark, for picking up the pieces to help finish the photography. I'm deeply grateful for all your hard work and efforts.

Thank you, Vicky Enright, for sharing your beautiful illustrations for the book. Your artwork is truly a gift.

To my amazing staff, whom I fondly call "the Fleurettes," this project would not have been possible without you. You've all been by my side, cheering me along the way, despite the long hours and numerous interruptions at the shop. I'm forever grateful for your support and dedication.

To Félicie, my digital manager, who jumped in and worked her magic. You helped me navigate all of the photography shot in France, kept me organized and on track with all that we had to do, and enhanced the layout edits by putting all my crazy design ideas in nice, neat folders to find. *Merci mille fois.*

To all my friends and colleagues in France, *merci* for opening up your homes, businesses, and hearts to me. You never hesitated to indulge my obsessive desire to get the right light for the photographs, the right flowers and containers for the arrangements, and so much more. Thank you, Teddy, Hassan from Sahn Drive, Florence of La Bruyère, and Adrienne and Myra from L'Arrosoir.

I am so grateful to my many American friends who contributed to this book. This includes the local flower growers and floral wholesalers who provided me with exquisite blooms and my friend Emily Kontos from The Thrifted Table, for always having an extra vintage plate or two to use in our photoshoots.

To Sharon Santoni, my dear friend and mentor, thank you for so generously sharing your home, garden, and wisdom. I deeply admire you and thank you for inspiring me every day.

Last, but not least, I want to say an enormous thank you to my husband, Scott, and our five loving boys—Cameron, Mitchell, Caleb, Zachary, and Jayden. Without all of you, this project would not have been possible. You never let me give up on this flower-filled dream. I know how blessed I am to have you in my life. Thank you for all your support. I love you with all my heart.

First published in the United States of America in 2023
by Rizzoli International Publications, Inc.
300 Park Avenue South
New York, NY 10010
www.rizzoliusa.com

All photography by Kindra Clineff, with the exception of

Paige Clark: pages 68, 69, 74, 75, 176, 178, 179
Abigail Matses: pages 50, 70, 78 (top left), 86–87, 94, 96–97, 171, 172, 174–175

Anne Soulier: front cover, endpapers, pages 2, 20, 21, 43, 49 (top left), 53, 54, 60–61, 62, 67, 73, 88, 89, 112, 121, 122, 146, 150, 154, 166, 168, 185, 186, 189, 190, 192 (bottom)

Illustrations by Vicky Enright

PROP CREDITS
Emily Kontos of The Thrifted Table: pages 90, 108, 110, 153
L'Arrosoir: page 190 (bouquet)

STYLING CREDITS
Abby Matses: pages: 68–69, 70–71, 74–75, 171

Publisher: Charles Miers
Editor: Sandra Gilbert Freidus
Editorial Assistance: Natalie Danford, Hilary Ney, and Tricia Levi
Design: Jan Derevjanik
Design Assistance: Olivia Russin
Production Manager: Maria Pia Gramaglia
Managing Editor: Lynn Scrabis

Printed in China

2023 2024 2025 2026 / 10 9 8 7 6 5 4 3 2

ISBN: 978-0-8478-9906-7
Library of Congress Control Number: 2022947569

Visit us online:
Facebook.com/RizzoliNewYork
instagram.com/rizzolibooks
twitter.com/Rizzoli_Books
pinterest.com/rizzolibooks
youtube.com/user/RizzoliNY
issuu.com/Rizzoli

ABOUT THE AUTHOR

SANDRA SIGMAN has designed French-inspired florals for hundreds of weddings and events at Les Fleurs, the French-style floral, home, and garden shop she opened in Andover, Massachusetts, in 1989. She became enchanted with flowers as a young girl while helping to create bouquets for her mother's home-based floral business. She later fell in love with France when she moved to Paris in the mid-1980s to skate professionally with Holiday on Ice. It was in the City of Light that she learned her signature style of arranging flowers from her favorite Parisian florist shop near her apartment. Through annual workshops at Les Fleurs and in France, she now shares her love of France and all things floral with others. Due to her floral expertise and engaging personality, Sandra has been featured in myriad magazines, including *Boston Magazine*, *Flower Magazine*, *New England Home*, *Northshore Magazine*, and *The Cottage Journal*. She has been featured on WCVB-TV Channel 5's Chronicle and has spoken at garden clubs across the country. For the past two years, she has exhibited annually at the prestigious Newport Flower Show in Rhode Island, where in 2018, she won first prize for Best New Vendor Home & Garden Marketplace. Sandra lives in Andover with her husband and their Cavachon and store mascot, Obie. The couple also has a pied-à-terre in Paris and a weekend home in Vermont.

ABOUT THE CO-AUTHOR

Victoria Abbott Riccardi is a journalist and book author who lived in Paris from 1982 to 1983 to study French cuisine at Le Cordon Bleu. For nearly twenty-five years, she has written travel, food, gardening, home, and lifestyle articles for various consumer print and online media in the United States and abroad, including *Bon Appétit*, *Condé Nast Traveller*, *Hemispheres*, and *The New York Times*. In 2003 she wrote the travel memoir *Untangling My Chopsticks: A Culinary Sojourn in Kyoto* (Broadway), a *New York Times* 2003 Notable Book excerpted in *Best Food Writing 2003* (Marlowe & Company). She has contributed to five other culinary and travel books. As a result of her work, she has appeared on national television several times, including on the *Food Network's Iron Chef America*, where she was a judge for the first (2004–2005) and second (2005–2006) seasons, CBS's *The Early Show*, and MSNBC's *Morning Blend*.

ABOUT THE FOREWORD WRITER

SHARON SANTONI grew up in England, but married a Frenchman and has raised their family in Normandy, France. She created the blog and brand My French Country Home and has written books on French living. Her websites and lifestyle magazine draw readers from around the world, many of whom subscribe to My French Country Home Box or purchase from her online boutique that carries all things French. She also welcomes an international clientele on her tours and shows them an authentic side of France that tourists rarely encounter.

ABOUT THE PHOTOGRAPHERS

Photographer KINDRA CLINEFF's enthusiasm for chasing light and capturing life in her images led to working engagements with national and international advertising, editorial, and corporate clients. During her thirty-five-year career as a professional photographer, she regularly produced feature assignments for publications such as *Better Homes and Gardens*, *Country Gardens*, *Country Home*, *The Cottage Journal*, and *Yankee*. Kindra partnered with writers, interior decorators, and culinary artists on numerous books, including *The Garden in Every Sense and Season* (Timber Press, 2018), *Farmhouse Modern* (Abrams/Stewart, Tabori & Chang, 2013) and *The New Terrarium* (Clarkson Potter/Random House, 2009). She lived with her partner, Tim, in Topsfield, Massachusetts, until her untimely death in 2022.

ANNE SOULIER is a French photographer, writer, and stylist. She took up photography after her children were born in order to hold onto moments and freeze time. Her early work focused on the ephemeral. For the past ten years, she has worked for French and international clients on brands for which she serves as artistic director. While fostering a timeless aesthetic, she creates simple, soft images in natural light, because she firmly believes in the power of beauty. She manages projects with one objective: to evoke emotion through imagery.

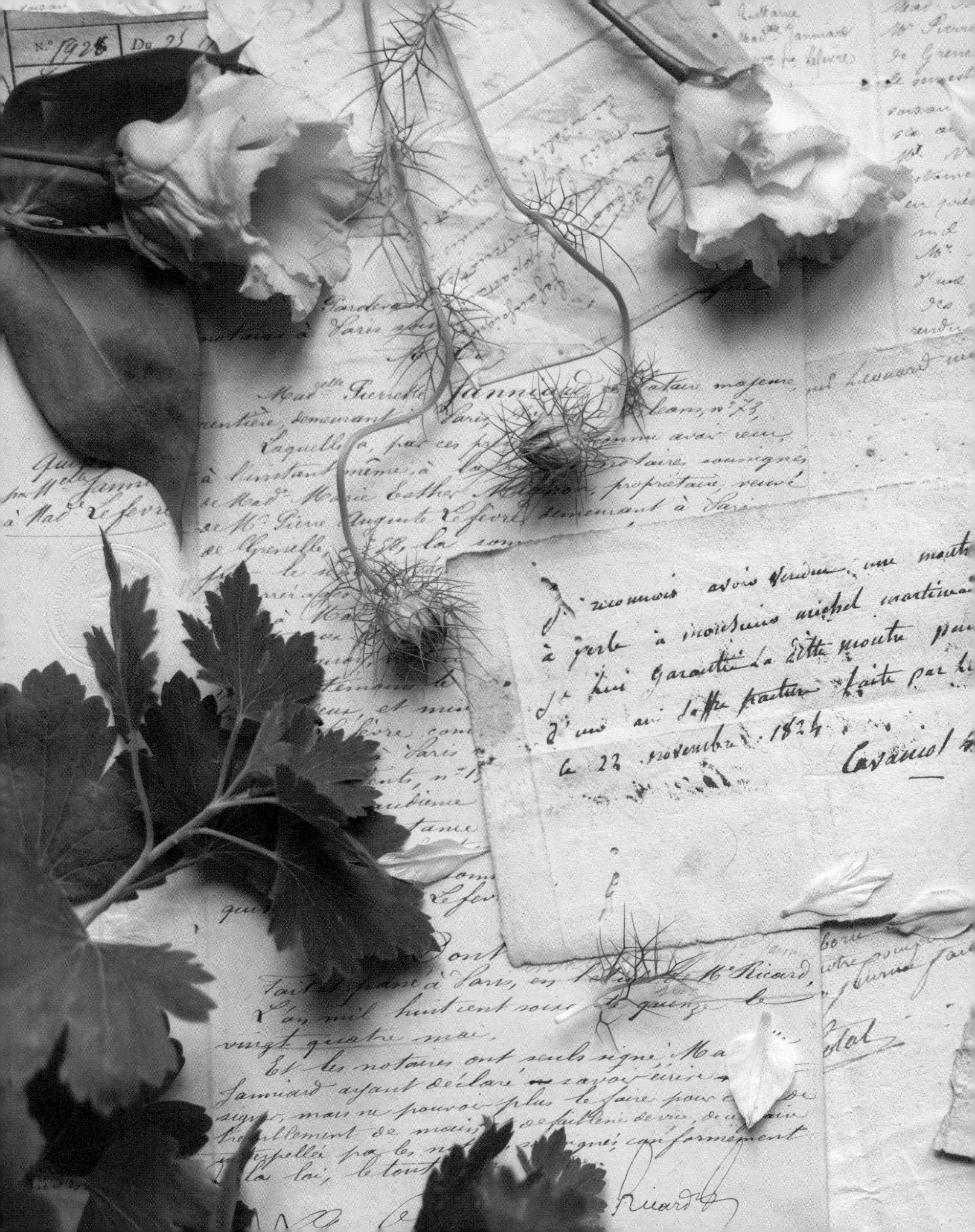